Traditional

READING PROGRAM FOR KIDS

MARILYN MARTYN

Illustrated by Chris Emmerson

Marilyn Martyn c/- Intertype Unit 45, 125 Highbury Road
BURWOOD VIC 3125
www.intertype.com.au

Ordering Information:
Quantity sales. Special discounts are available on quantity purchases by corporations, associations, and others. For details, contact the "Special Sales Department" at the address above.

Reading Program for Kids / Marilyn Martyn —1st ed. ISBN 978-0-6487977-7-7

THIS BOOK IS DEDICATED TO

SOLON

JENNIFER AND CHRIS

without whom it would not exist

CONTENTS

Preface

This book is a resource for parents and caregivers of a child learning to read.

It contains ideas for activities to share with a child. It outlines the primary phonics and skills needed in the early years of learning to read.

The KEY ingredients for effective early reading instruction are: step by step instruction in:

- Phonemic or sound Awareness
- Knowledge of letter-sound relationships known as phonics
- Reading accessible texts where words are easy to sound out and are parts of a young child's vocabulary.

The FOCUS is on all three.

I present the ***reading*** skills taught in the first three years of formal schooling.

Children develop these skills at their pace. It is best if you work patiently with your child and consolidate their progress step-by-step.

Functional imaging has enabled neuroscientists to look inside the human brain. It is comprised of billions of interconnected brain cells.

Reading and writing build up connections within the brain.

- These are called reading circuits.
- Reading circuits are formed in the left hemisphere of the brain.
- They also connect with other areas in the brain.
- It takes time and practise for these circuits to form.

Reading is, therefore, a whole-brain activity. All brains are unique because everyone builds their brain connections.

When teaching a young child to read, a multi-sensory approach works best.
A multi-sensory approach means using kinesthetic (physical), audio and visual activities to build reading circuits.

Three Reading Behaviour Checklists in the Appendix will enable you to measure your child's progress.

About the Author

Marilyn trained as a teacher-librarian specializing in children's literature and developed a career around her love of books and reading.

She also spent some time as an education consultant for two publishers, visiting many schools.

Marilyn has taught English and mathematics to children from the beginning grade to year nine in secondary schools.

She found many opportunities to teach children who had difficulty learning to read. She taught many students in schools and still does as a private tutor.

After sitting with many frustrated students who did not know how to decode (sound out) words, Marilyn devised a series of lessons that gave them the ability to sound out words quickly.

These lessons are the foundation of this book.

Modern reading research has shown the crucial role of phonics in learning to read.

Early, systematic and explicit teaching of how to hear the sounds in words, and how to sound out words is vital in the early stages of learning to read.

Marilyn is eager to share her knowledge and experience.

She wants as many children as possible to become fluent readers and writers.

Introduction

This book gives you a simple step-by-step way to help your child link the way sounds are written in English with the words heard every day.

I outline phonics, a proven method of teaching reading based on phonetics (the science dealing with speech sounds).

I avoid the phonetic symbols and terminology and use words and items with which readers and their families will be familiar.

I show you the methods I used over many years. They will help you to consolidate the lessons your child receives at school.

I will explain each skill and how you can help your child to improve steadily, step by step.

I wrote this material in a straight forward way. Reading and spelling go hand in hand. You will see your child's spelling and reading improve when you help him, or her do the writing exercises with the reading exercises.

The lessons will take you and your child from the most accessible parts of English words to the more complex ones.

Take your time with each lesson, and you will develop your child's ability to read, write and spell English fluently.

The four aspects of reading and spelling skills are :

- **Phonics:** The relationships between letters and sounds.
- **Fluency:** The ability to read quickly and naturally, recognize words automatically, and group words rapidly.
- **Vocabulary knowledge:** Remembering new words and what they mean.
- **Text comprehension:** Processing what is being read and developing higher-order thinking skills.

This book will help your child develop all four areas.

The lessons will help your child to learn:

- The sounds of English and the combinations of letters that represent them.
- How to blend sounds into words and how to spell them.
- How to recognize new words when they see them.
- The spelling patterns for English words.
- To read sentences: starting with simple ones.
- I provide harder examples later on.

Your child will receive a thorough grounding in the basics.

This book is for:

- Parents of children with reading difficulties who want to give their child extra help or an earlier start with learning to read.
- Parents of children diagnosed with dyslexia.
- Adults who want to improve their understanding of English texts by revising phonics.
- Students who are learning English as a second language.

Steady mastering of the foundation reading skills outlined in this book will lead to

READING FREEDOM!

One of the essential pre-reading skills your child must master is sound or phonemic awareness.

Phonemic or sound Awareness includes:

- Recognizing words contain several individual sounds.
- The ability to recognize and change sounds in words.
- It is a predictor of early reading success.

Background Knowledge:

- Phonemes are the smallest units of sound in a language.
- Children need to hear the phonemes in a language to learn to read, write and spell.
- Words contain a collection of phonemes.
- Phonemes are also called sounds.
- There are around **44** phonemes in English.
- Phonemic Awareness is the term that indicates a child is, or is not, attuned to the different sounds in spoken language.
- Phonemic Awareness enables a child to listen for patterns in words that sound the same and to break words into syllables, onsets and rimes.
- Syllables are units of speech often heard as one sound.
- A syllable is a collectionof sounds.
- A syllable has to contain a vowel sound.
- Syllables have an onset and rime.
- The onset is the consonant sound/s before the vowel.
- The rime is the rest of the syllable, including the vowel sound.
- An example: read is a one-syllable word. The vowel sound is **/e/** spelled **'ea'.** The onset is **/r/** and the rime is **/ead/.**
- Donkey is a two-syllable word: d-on+k-ey. 2 rimes and 2 onsets.

PHONEMIC OR SOUND AWARENESS ACTIVITIES

The following <u>phonemic awareness activities</u> will help your child become attuned to the sounds of language.

The oral activities outlined are:

- Rhyme and alliteration
- Blending word parts
- Clapping syllables in words
- Counting sounds in words
- Segmenting sounds in words
- Identifying the difference between a sound and a word
- Separating beginning, middle and ending sounds in words

Activity 1: Sound discrimination

Select a sound you want your child to hear.

Have a list of words that include your target sound at the beginning as well as some non-targeted words. Say each word slowly.

Ask your child to clap when they hear the sound. For example, bag, dog, ball, did, do, digs.

You can ask for vowel and consonant sounds and blends.

Say the words and ask the child to listen to how they say each word. Stretch out the sounds.

An example: **b** (onset) **ath** (rime) **bath**

Activity 2: Collect a number of pictures from magazines and paste onto card.

Examples, dog, man, girl, tree.

Discuss beginning sounds, middlesoundsand end sounds. Ask: What word begins with the sound **/g/**? What word has the **/a/** sound in the middle? What word ends with the **/l/**sound?

Activity 3: Use children's stories to play with speech sounds.

Use books with:

- **Rhyme** – words with the same ending: phone - alone, peach - beach
- **Alliteration** – words starting with the same sound: A greedy green grasshopper
- **Assonance** – words with the same vowel sound:
  Examples: bug snug rug tug

BOOKS WITH RHYME

Each Peach Pear Plum: Janet and Alan Ahlberg (Puffin Books 1986)

This Little Chick: John Lawrence (2002)

Madeline (Madeline Series) Ludwig Bemelmans (1939)

A Giraffe and a Half: Shel Silverstein (Harper Collins 1964)

The Cat in the Hat (Beginner Books) (Random House)

BOOKS WITH ALLITERATION

Animalia: by Graeme Base (Abrams, 1986)

Dr Seuss's ABC: by Dr Seuss (Random House, 1963)

Alligator Arrived with Apples: A Potluck Alphabet Feast by Crescent Dragonwagon and Jose Aruego (1992)

READ ALOUD STORIES

Where is the Green Sheep: Mem Fox and Judy Horacek (Penguin Books, 2004)

The Foot Book: Dr Seuss (2018)

Hand, Hand, Fingers, Thumb: Al Perkins (1969)

Will You Read to Me: Denys Cazet. (2008)

The Magic Hat: Mem Fox (2003)

Activity 4: Letters and Sounds

Collect some objects. (***For example*** - fork, pen, book, doll, toy,). Say the beginning sound and ask your child to match the object and write the beginning letter.

Don't mention the letter's name, only the sound it represents. If your child says the letter name, acknowledge it, and then ask for the sound it makes. Children can get letter names and the sounds they represent mixed up.

Activity 5: Naming

You will need a large blank project book.

Paste or draw a picture at the top of each page.

Examples: (ball, fish, glass, hat, pig, sun, top).

Your child can either draw or find pictures of objects with a name that rhymes with the illustration. Discuss the middle and ending sounds of each word.

Write the words under each illustration.

Activity 6: Rhyming Game

Ask what rhymes with a given word?

For example, clock, bird, toy, sun

Fold a piece of paper in half. Ask your child to draw two things whose names rhyme.

An example: **cat/hat**.

Activity 7: Sound Boxes

No Writing Necessary

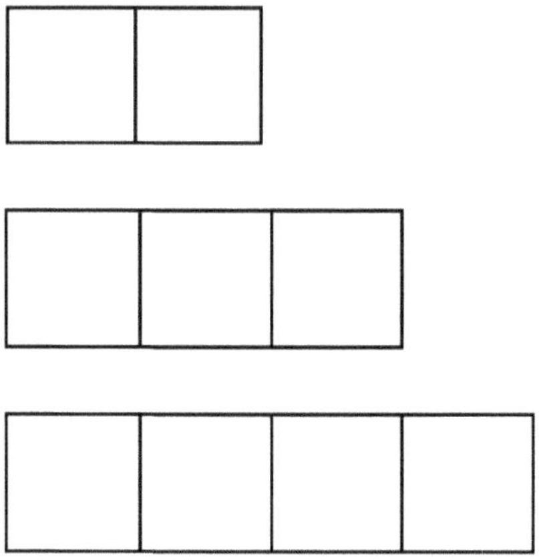

Draw the boxes on stiff cardboard. Have some counters to fit each box.

Say a word. Your child chooses one of the sound boxes and lines the counters below each box. They move a counter up into a box saying the sound as they do so beginning from the left box. They then blend the sounds into a word again.

bad (3)	ship (3)	fly (3)	news (2)
best (4)	camp (4)	way (2)	left (4)
boy (2)	swim (4)	cook (3)	in (2)
cap (3)	cream (4)	left (4)	we (2)
as (2)	clock (4)	new (2)	up (2)
at (2)	no (2)	shed (3)	sea (2)
hat (3)	girl (3)	sick (3)	wing (3)
under (4)	sky (3)	hard (3)	set (3)

Activity 8: Counting the Sounds in Words

The words below have a consonant-vowel-consonant pattern.

bag but bus cat did dog fat fox got had hat his hot let run six sun ten tin pig

Ask your child to say a word and clap the number of sounds in it. Blend them together again. An example, **(bag /b-a-g/ bag).**

Activity 9: Deleting Sounds

Say **moonbeam** without **moon**.

Say **pancake** without **pan**.

Say **rainbow** without **rain**.

Say **sunshine** without **sun**.

Deleting the first phoneme in a word.

Say **clap** then without the **/c/.**

Say **slack** then without **/s/.**

Say **spin** then without **/s/.**

Say **pin** then without **/p/.**

Say **grain** then without **/g/.**

Say **clock** then without the **/c/.**

Deleting the first syllable in a word.

Say **person** without **per**.

Say **whistle** without **whis**.

Say **goanna** without **go**.

Say **handle** without **han**.

Say **hockey** without **hock**.

Say **grandpa** without **grand**.

Say **hermit** without **her.**

Say **daffodil** without **daff.**

Deleting the last phoneme in a blend.

Say **fast** without **/t/.**

Say **pond** without **/d/.**

Say **pant** without **/t/.**

Say **bend** without **/d/.**

Say **spelt** without **/t/.**

Say **wind** without **/d/.**

Say **spent** without **/t/.**

Say **last** without **/t/**.

Phonemic Awareness

There are **FIVE** basic phonemic awareness tasks. They are:

1. The ability to hear rhymes and alliteration.
2. The ability to hear different beginning sounds in words.
3. The ability to blend words and split the syllables in words.
4. The ability to separate all the sounds in words and blend them again.
5. The ability to replace beginning sounds with a new sound to make a new word. It is called phonemic manipulation.

If your child has difficulty with the phonemic awareness exercises, this may cause an issue with learning to read.

Make sure your child's hearing and eyesight are within natural limits. Many children have been labelled with a learning disability when the problem was a sight or hearing issue.

Phonemic Awareness is the preparation for learning to read and spell.

A Phonogram Checklist is available in the appendix.

Letter - Sound Relationships

When we speak, we join sounds together to make words. All people who speak our language agree on the meaning of the words.
We form these words into sentences.

There are two sound groups in English.

1. **Vowel** sounds
2. **Consonant** sounds
3. English uses **18 vowel sounds,** and **25 consonant sounds** to make words.

Words are a collection of vowel and consonant sounds blended together.
Every word must have at least one vowel sound.

A **syllable** is a word, or part of a word, with only one vowel sound. Most English words have two or more syllables.

We use the **26 letters** in the English alphabet to represent the **18 vowel sounds** and **25 consonant sounds** used to form words.

The English Alphabet has 26 letters to spell around 44 sounds.
One, two, three and sometimes four letters are used to spell sounds in words.
Some letters spell more than one sound.
English vowel sounds may be spelled in several ways.

87% of English words follow English spelling rules. About13% don't, usually, because a vowel sound has a different spelling.

Read and Write the following most used words.

They will become recognised as **sight words.** Many can be sounded out.

a	and	he	I
in	is	it	of
that	the	to	was
all	are	as	at
be	but	for	had
have	him	his	not
on	one	said	so
they	we	with	you
about	an	back	been
before	big	by	call
came	can	come	could
did	do	down	first
from	get	go	has
her	here	if	into
just	like	little	look
made	make	more	me
much	must	my	no
new	now	off	old
only	or	other	our
out	over	right	see
she	some	their	them
then	there	this	two
up	want	well	went
were	what	when	where
which	who	will	your

An Example of a Lesson Plan

Once your child recognizes consonant, and short vowel letter-sound relationships prepare a fifteen minutes daily lesson.

(Vowels a e i o u   Consonants   b c d f g h j k l m n p q r s t v w x y z)

Once they know these phonemes, they will be able to read and write many words.

Include in each lesson:

1. **Alphabet Review**: Continue to review letter-sound relationships.
2. **Reading Words**: The aim is to develop instant recognition of words (both sight words and decodable words).
3. Reading **short sentences** containing words studied.
4. Sentence **writing** by the child.
5. **Spelling:** selected from words used in the current lesson.

Lesson Example

Alphabet Review: lower case short vowel sound.   **a** e i o u

What is the letter name? What is its sound? The /a/ sound as in cat.

One-Syllable Words

Dan	**man**	**fan**	**can**	**pan**	**pat**	**at**	**an**

Ask your child to think of some words. Write them on the whiteboard.

Sight Words

because	**there**	**my**	**was**	**to**	**were**

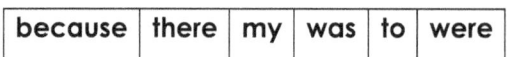

Write the words on cards for frequent revising.

Sentences

- Jim and Jan ran to the park.
- Dan and his dog were there.

Spelling

Writing words and sentences is essential. Remember to teach punctuation.

Practise writing sight words from memory.

Introduce the graded texts in this book as soon as possible.

Handwriting

Emphasize neat, legible handwriting.

Handwriting is related to reading and spelling abilities.

Handwriting Suggestions

- Use a whiteboard with 3 horizontal lines to show your child how to write a letter.
- Write letters on the line. Explain how they vary above or below the line.
- Write large letters. Your child will develop fine motor skills later.
- Encourage them to write the letter in the air a few times.
- Then on the line on the whiteboard.
- Have a sizeable unlined project book for the child to write in.
- You draw 3 lines on each page. Make sure the pencil is sharp.
- When the child is writing, make sure the area around them is free from clutter.

How they sit is relevant.

They need to have.

- Hips against the back of the chair.
- Feet flat on the floor pointing forward.
- Back straight, head high. A straight back allows this.
- One hand holds the pencil resting on the middle finger and holding it with the thumb and forefinger.
- The other hand holds the paper as needed.

a b c d e f g h I j k l m n o p

q r s t u v w x y z

A B C D E F G H I J K L M N

O P Q R S T U V W X Y

Writing Lower Case Letters

a b c d e f g h i j k l m o p q r s t u v w x y z

A circle or line or a combination of both are used to form letters.

Letters that begin at two on the clock face.

a b **c** **d** e **f** **g** h i j k l m n **o** p **q** r **s** t u v w x y z

For example, Letter a. Begin the circle beginning at two on the clock face and draw it stopping close to 2.

Move the pencil upwards just past the outline of the circle then straight down just below the shape of the circle.

Practice drawing the letter **a** in the air. Relax arm and fingers at the same time.

Write rows of **a** on a whiteboard or paper. Make sure each letter rests on the line.

Once you start at 2:00, it is easy to follow the shape of the letter.

The other letters which start at 2:00 on the clock are: **c d f g o q s**

Letters that begin with lines

b e h i j k l m n p r t u v w x y

Concentrate on forming easily recognizable letters.

Upper Case Letters

A B C D E F G H I J K L M N O P Q R S T U V W X Y Z

All UPPER-CASE LETTERS are tall.

They almost fill the space between two lines.

Upper case letters beginning at 2:00.

C G O Q S

Upper case letters beginning with a line.

A B D E F H I J K L M N P R S

Practise writing the **UPPER CASE** or **CAPITAL LETTERS.**

In the beginning, ask your child to describe what they are doing as they write each letter.

Outline of Lessons

Lesson 1: The Alphabet

THE ALPHABET

The English Alphabet has 26 letters. They each have a name.

The name given to each letter in English is like the sound it represents. Be sure your child does not confuse the letter names with sounds.

Upper Case or Capital Letters

A B C D E F G H I J K L M N O P Q R S T U V W X YZ

Lower Case Letters

a b c d e f g h i j k l m n o p q r s t u v w x y z

The Vowel Letters are

a e i o u and sometimes y and r

The Consonant Letters are

b c d f g h j k l m n p q r s t v w x y z

Exercise:

Make sure your child understands that letters have names and are used to spell sounds. Check if your child recognizes the sound each single letters spells.

You may decide to do the lesson using letters and sounds rather than letter names. You can come back later and do it with letter names.

Help your child to learn the letters by name or sound and their position in the alphabet. Explain alphabetical order and how it is used in a dictionary or phone book.

Say the letter and ask your child to write it in upper or lower case form.

Make cards of **UPPER CASE** and **LOWER CASE** letters. Your child can use them to match upper and lower case letters, put letters in alphabetical order and memorize the sound each letter represents.

NOTE q has two sounds, **/k/** and **/w/** and has the letter as a companion **(qu).**
/x/ has two sounds, **/k/** and **/s/.**

The Alphabet - Lower Case Letters

a	b	c	d
e	f	g	h
i	j	k	l
m	n	o	p
q	r	s	t
u	v	w	x
y	z	***Lower Case Letters***	

The Alphabet—Upper Case Letters

A	B	C	D
E	F	G	H
I	J	K	L
M	N	O	P
Q	R	S	T
U	V	W	X
Y	Z	**Upper Case Letters**	

Lesson 2: Sounds

English, like other languages, has two categories of sounds.

Vowel Sounds: Vowel sounds are voiced, causing the vocal cords to vibrate. The sound passes freely through the mouth. Vowels add volume to speech.

Consonant Sounds: Consonant sounds are made by touching mouthparts together. Some consonants are also voiced using the vocal cords, and some are not. Consonants are hard to separate from vowels.

We blend **vowel sounds** and **consonant sounds** to form words. Every word has to contain at least one vowel sound.

Syllables

Syllables are parts of words that contain a vowel sound. If a word has one vowel sound, it has one syllable. If a word has more than one vowel sound, it may have two, three or more syllables.

Most English words have two or more syllables.

rab/bit	**Sat/ur/day**	**be/cause**	**be/gan**
2 syllables	3 syllables	2 syllables	2 syllables

Lesson 3: Sounds of the English Language

18 Vowel Sounds		*25 Consonant Sounds*	
Sound	*Key Word*	*Sound*	*Key Word*
/ă/	apple	/b/	boy
/ĕ/	egg	/d/	dog
/i/	Indian	/f/	frog
/ŏ/	orange	/h/	hat
/ŭ/	umbrella	/g/	girl
/āe/	make	/j/	jet
/ēe/	feet	/k/	kite
/īe/	pie	/l/	lion
/ōe/	coat	/m/	monkey
/ūe/	flute	/n/	net
/air/	stair	/p/	pig
/ar/	bar car pa	/r/	rabbit
/er/	fern, bird, hurt	/s/	sun
/oi/	boil boy	/t/	turtle
/ŏŏ/	book	/v/	van
/oo/	soon	/w/	watch
/or/	for	/y/	yacht
/ow/	cow house	/x/	fox
		/z/	zip
		/ch/	chip
		/ng/	sing
		/qu/	quit

<table>
<tr><td rowspan="5">English also has the schwa sound.
The schwa sound is a vowel sound
spoken softly, and it sounds like
/uh/ or /er/.
It is the most common vowel sound.

Examples

away (uhway)
over (ovuh)
doctor (doctuh)
Dinosaur (dinersaur)</td><td>/sh/</td><td>ship</td></tr>
<tr><td>/th/ unvoiced</td><td>thin</td></tr>
<tr><td>/th/ voiced</td><td>them</td></tr>
<tr><td>/zh/</td><td>vision</td></tr>
<tr><td colspan="2"></td></tr>
</table>

Exercise:

Read through the chart.

- Say some words and listen to the sounds they contain to prepare for teaching your child.
- What is the vowel sound or vowel sounds in each word?
- Listen carefully to how you say them.
- Take note of the mouthparts (tongue, teeth and lips) you use?
- Place fingers on your throat and feel the sound made from the larynx (vocal cords).
- Notice how you use your breath.

Encourage your child to do this with simple words or words she or he knows.

Sound or phonemic awareness is a foundation stage so take your time.

REVISION

PHONEMIC (SOUND) AWARENESS ACTIVITIES

A child has phonemic awareness if they are aware of the sounds in words. They will hear individual sounds in words and be able to change them around. Phonemic awareness is not phonics.

Phonics deals with the relationships between sounds and the letters that spell them.

Your child's literacy development is enhanced by reading to him or her daily.

Be sure to provide a print-rich environment. Reading stories together should be as free and uninterrupted as possible.

Phonemic awareness activities should be oral. Do them often in short bursts and make them fun.
The following is what your child should be able to do.

1. **Hear rhymes and alliteration (rhyming words).**
   Activity: Read nursery rhymes and short poems and stories that contain rhyming words. Ask your child to tell you the words that rhyme.
2. **Notice how words begin with different sounds.**
   Activity: Show some pictures (example: sit, sun, man). Ask which image begins with a different sound?
3. **Blend the sounds in words and split them up.**
   Activity: Say the first sound in a word and then the rest of the word. An example is f – ast. Ask your child to tell you the word. Say a word and get your child to clap the syllables. (hap/py — two claps). Break words up into their sounds.

1. **Hear the individual sounds in words.**
   Activity: say a word your child knows slowly. Ask them to tell you the sounds in the word. (Example: **/m//a//t/**.

2. **Replace sounds in one word to make a different word.**
   Activity: Say the word **dog**. Replace the first sound **/d/** with **/l/**. What is the new word?

If your child finds these activities difficult, don't panic but speak to a child specialist about it. It can be a warning sign that he or she may experience difficulty learning to read and write.

Successful reading begins with phonemic or sound awareness and recognition of the letters of the alphabet.

Reading and writing should go hand in hand. Incorporate as many writing activities as possible in your lessons.

The following activities will support your child's mastery of words.

- Drawing objects and writing names.
- Writing word families and drawing pictures.
- Writing action words (verbs) and drawing or doing the action.
- Copying a nursery rhyme from a book.
- Filling in missing letters in words using a whiteboard. Kids love doing this.
- Looking at a picture and writing the names of things in it.
- Writing short sentences. Write them on card then cut out each word. Put the sentences together again.
- Drawing pictures for a word in a sentence. Example: Sit in the (**PICTURE OF A CHAIR**) Jack.

Lesson 4: How Sounds are Spelled in Words

This lesson outlines the vowel and consonant sounds.

About 87% of English words follow the accepted spelling rules. Around 13% may contain at least one irregularly spelled vowel sound. Understanding the spelling of vowel sounds helps with reading, writing and spelling.

5 Short Vowel Sounds:

ant **e**gg **i**nk n**o**t b**u**t

5 Long Vowel Sounds:

c**a**ke f**ee**t p**ie** b**oa**t r**u**de

The long vowel sounds in English have more than one spelling.

Diphthongs or Gliding Vowels:

When two vowel sounds in a syllable are combined they are quickly spoken to make it seem like one sound.

Examples:

r**ou**nd/h**ow** **oi**l/b**oy** h**au**l/j**aw**

The sounds have more than one spelling.

Vowel Digraphs

A digraph is **two letters** used to spell one sound.

The digraph **OO** is a vowel digraph (two letters used to spell one sound) which represent a short sound and a longsound:

Long sound: **soon** Short sound: **look**

Vowel Digraphs — r-controlled vowel sounds:

t**ur**n f**er**n b**ir**d p**ar**k f**or**k

Consonant Sounds

(one letter spells one sound)

b c d f g h j k l m n p q r s t v w x y z

bed **c**at **d**og **f**at **g**et **h**ot **j**ug **k**id **l**ap **m**an **n**et **p**ig **r**at **s**un **t**ap **v**an **w**in **y**ell **z**ip

q is also a consonant, but it has two sounds /**k**//**w**/ and has **u** as a companion (**qu**it)

x is also a consonant, but it has 2 sounds /**k**//**s**/ **ks** (fo**x**)

The Consonant Digraphs

(two letters spell one sound) chop s **sh**ip **th**in **th**is **wh**ip si**ng**

Lesson 5: Short Vowel Sounds

The first sounds to learn are **short vowel sounds.**

Sound	Word
/a/	apple
/e/	egg
/i/	Indian
/o/	orange
/u/	umbrella

Exercise:

Think of other simple words that contain the short vowel sounds. Here are some to start with:

b**a**t m**a**t s**e**t l**e**t b**i**t k**i**d l**o**t g**o**t f**u**n s**u**n

Ask your child to say the words and listen for the short vowel sounds. Write the words down as the child tells them.

Photocopy the table of the five short vowel sounds below.

Glue it onto cardboard.

Cut the chart into 15 same-sized cards.

Place them face up. Ask the child to match each sound, picture and word.

Use the cards for the memory game.

Memory Game (for one or two people)

- Place each card face down.
- Each player takes a turn to turn one card face up.
- The short vowel sound, a word with that vowel sound or the name of the picture, is spoken.
- Place it face down again.
- Pick up another card and do the same.

If a player remembers where a matching card is, he or she can turn it up and leave both cards face up and try to find the third card. If they do, these cards are removed from the game. The person with the most cards wins.

/a/		**a**pple
/e/		**e**gg
/i/		**I**ndian
/o/	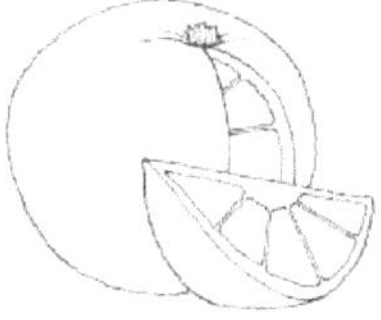	**o**range
/u/		**u**mbrella

Lesson 6: Consonant Sounds

Consonant sounds spelt with a single letter:

b c d f g h j k l m n p q r s t v w x y z

The letters **c** and **g** can each represent two different consonant sounds.

The letter **c** can sound /**k**/ as in **c**at or /**s**/ as in **c**ent

The letter **g** can sound /**g**/ as in **g**irl or /**j**/ as in **g**em

We blend consonant sounds and vowel sounds to form words.

Consonant sounds do not make a word unless they have at least one vowel sound with them. **All words must contain at leastone vowel sound.**

Activity:

Photocopy the chart of the consonant sounds, pictures and words from the following pages.

You can also make a chart together. Pictures can be found online or in old magazines, or you can draw them. Make sure every square is the same size.

Cut apart the sound, picture and word.

Ask your child to match the sound, the picture and the word.

Find some old magazines and cut out pictures beginning with each consonant sound.

In a blank project book, label the pages with the letters of the alphabet and help him or her to sort the pictures and glue them on the correct pages.

For example, a picture of a dog would be added to /**d**/ page. Place a bird under /**b**/ or the name of a bird under the letter of its name.

Say that **dog**, for instance, begins with a consonant sound **/d/.** Ask: Can you think of other **'d'** words?

Ask your child to say the beginning sound of what's in each picture throughout the book. Keep adding photos to this book to consolidate their knowledge.

Ask him or her to say the beginning sound of what's in each picture throughout the book. Keep adding illustrations to this book to consolidate your child's knowledge.

See if you both can invent a consonant game.

/b/		**b**oy
/c/		**c**at
/d/		**d**og
/f/		**f**rog

/**g**/		**g**irl
/**h**/		**h**at
/**j**/	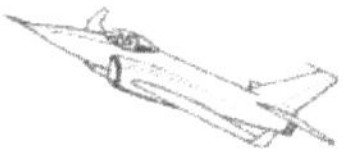	**j**et
/**k**/	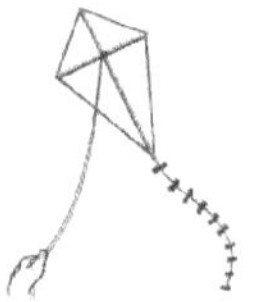	**k**ite
/**l**/		**l**ion

/m/		monkey
/n/	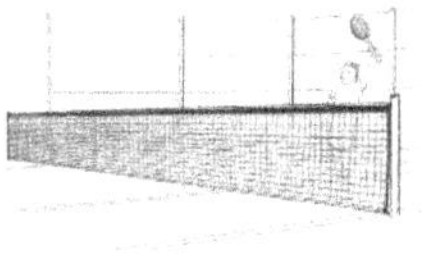	net
/p/		pig
/r/		rat
/s/	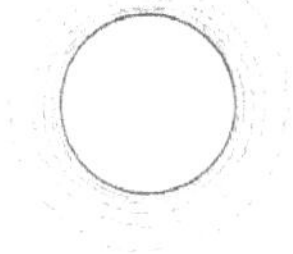	Sun
/t/		tree

/**v**/		**v**an
/**w**/		**w**atch
/**x**/		fo**x**
/**y**/	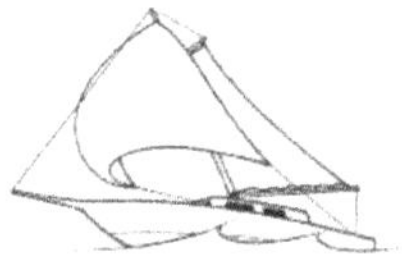	**y**acht
/**z**/		**z**ebra

Lesson 7: Making Words with Vowel and Consonant Sounds

Blending Short Vowels and Consonants

Say the vowel sound /**a**/ Say the consonant sound /**m**/
Blend them together to form the word, **am**

Say the vowel sound /**a**/ Say the consonant sound /**n**/
Blend them to form the word, **an**

Say the vowel sound /**a**/ Say the consonant sound /**s**/
Blend them to form the word, **as**

Say the vowel sound /**a**/ Say the consonant sound /**t**/
Blend them to form the word, **at**

Say the consonant sound /**n**/ Say the vowel sound /**a**/
Say the consonant sound /**n**/
Blend them to form the word, **Nan**

Say the consonant sound **/m/** Say the vowel sound **/a/**
Say the consonant sound **/n/**
Blend them to form the word, **man**

Say the consonant sound /**s**/ Say the vowel sound /**a**/

Say the consonant sound /**t**/

Blend them to form the word, **sat**

Ask your child to read and write the words. See if they can write more from memory:

am	**an**	**as**	**at**	**Nan***	**man**	**sat**

***Use** an upper case or capital letter when beginning a sentence or when writing a name.

Lesson 8: More Words with Short Vowel Sounds

When writing English, a sentence begins with a capital letter and finishes with a full stop **(.)** or a question mark **(?)** or an exclamation mark **(!)**.

Sight Words

Sight words are words that are not easy to decode.

You learn to recognize them on sight : examples: **I was the**

Short Vowel Sound /a/

at	am	an	as	sat	Sam	has	Nan	can	cat

Sam has a cat. Nan has a cat.

The cat sat on the mat.

Compose and write some short sentences together.

Short Vowel Sound /e/

net	pet	met	let	set	get	wet

Sam gets a pet. I met the pet.

Let the pet sit.

Compose and write some short sentences together.

Short Vowel Sound /i/

tip	sit	lit	bit	did	fig	gig	pig	big

The pig bit Sam. The pig did a jig.

Sam and the pig ate a fig.

Compose and write some short sentences together.

Short Vowel Sound /o/

hot	cot	dot	fog	log	nod	pot	rod	nod	dog

The hot dog sat on a log. The frog sat ona log.

Did the dog sit on the frog?

Compose and write some short sentences together.

Short vowel sound /u/

bug	dug	hug	rug	sun	bun	fun	jug	mug	tug

The bug sat on the bun. The mug was on the rug.

The bug had fun on the rug.

Makeup and write some short sentences together.

Read thesesentences:

Sam has a cat and a dog.

Nan has a cat and a dog.

Sam gets a pet dog and cat.

I met the pet dog at Sam's.

The pig bit Sam and Sam was sad.

The pig did a jig and ate the fig.

The hot dog sat on a log.

Sam and the hot dog jog.

The bug was on the rug.

Exercise:

- Help your child to remember and write as many three-letter words as possible.
- Remember that all words must contain a vowel sound.
- Help your child write some easy sentences with their three-letter words.
- Write the sentences on strips of cardboard. Cut out all words.
- Use the words to compose sentences and then write them.

Activity:

Photocopy the following letters and paste them on light cardboard.

Cut out each letter into the same sized rectangle.

Make three-letter words using the short vowel sounds. Write the words.

Examples, cat beg fin log bun

NOTE: q has two sounds /**k**//**w**/ and always has **u** as a companion.

x has two sounds /**k**//**s**/

I have used outlines for the letters so your child can colour them in. You can use your education authority's recommended script for this exercise.

a	b	c	d
e	f	g	h
i	j	k	l
m	n	o	p
q	r	s	t
u	v	w	x
y	z	**English Alphabet** ***Lower Case Letters***	

a	e	i	o	u	**Vowel** **Letters**

Lesson 9: 3 Letter Words with the CVC Pattern

(CVC means consonant- vowel -consonant sound pattern)

Read and write each word.

bad	sad	mad	lad	fad	dad	had	pad	sad	sat
let	bet	get	jet	met	set	ten	pen	net	pet
big	dig	fig	jig	pig	wig	rig	zip	fix	mix
lot	pot	cot	fog	log	dot	got	not	jot	top
rug	bug	dug	mug	tug	lug	fun	sun	hum	mud

Now read the following sentences.

The big lad is mad at dad.

Dad is mad at the bad lad.

Dad let the lad get a pet.

The pet sat on the mat.

The big dog sat in the mud.

The sun is hot.

The lad and dad had fun in the sun.

The dog and cat sat on the big rug.

The bug had fun in the mug.

The pig got a big fig.

Exercise:

Write all the words and sentences you have just read. Write five sentences of your own.

Fill-the–Gaps

big	*mad*	*is*	*the*	*bad*	*got*	*dog*	*mat*	*pig*	*in*	*hot*	*fun*	*sun*

Write the sentences with the correct words in place.

The ___ lad is ___ at dad. *(bad, mad)*

Dad __ mad at ___ bad lad. *(is, the)*

Dad ___ the lad a pet ___. *(got, dog)*

The pet ___ sat on the ___. *(dog, mat)*

The big ___ sat __ the mud. *(pig, in)*

The ___ is ___. *(sun, hot)*

The lad and dad had ___ in the ___.*(fun, sun)*

Lesson 10: ck

The two letters **'c'** and **'k'** spell the /**k**/ sound at the end of words with a short stressed vowel.

Ja**ck**	ti**ck**	si**ck**	ne**ck**
sa**ck**	Mi**ck**	ro**ck**	de**ck**
ta**ck**	li**ck**	do**ck**	pe**ck**
pa**ck**	pi**ck**	so**ck**	lu**ck**
ra**ck**	ki**ck**	lo**ck**	du**ck**

Jack and his sister were sick.

Tick–tock went the big clock.

Mick and Jack ran with the dog.

Pick up the pack of cards and play.

Kick the ball and get a goal.

Jack put the duck in the sack to carry it home.

Activity: Write as many 'ck' words as you can.

Contractions:

When two words combine to make a shorter word, the new word is called a **contraction**. An apostrophe (') goes where the letters are left out:

I am	**I'm**
you are	**you're**
she is	**she's**
he is	**he's**
would not	**wouldn't**
should not	**shouldn't**
could not	**couldn't**
they have	**they've**

Read these sentences:

I can't go to school today because I'm sick.

She isn't my sister.

He isn't my brother.

They've had lunch today.

I wouldn't eat too many sweets.

Lesson 11: Consonant Blends

Consonant Blends (also known as clusters) are two or more consonant sounds blended together.

Most **consonant blends** have only one spelling and can be recognized in the beginning, middle and end of words.

Below are consonant blends with short vowels and consonant sounds to form one-syllable words. Make cards for each blend for practise sessions.

Beginning Consonant Blends

bl br cl cr dr dw fl fr gl gr pl pr sc scr sk sl shr sm sn sp spl spr st str sw tr thr tw

Final Consonant Blends

ct dge ft lb ld lf lk lm lp lt mp nce nd ng nt nse nch nk pt sk sp st tch xt

Beginning Blends	Final Blends
black **br**an **cl**an **cr**am	a**ct** ba**dge** le**ft** bu**lb** we**ld**
drop **dw**ell	e**lf** wa**lk** fi**lm** ye**lp**
flat **fr**og **Gl**en **gr**ab **Gw**en	me**lt** ca**mp**
plant **pr**int **sc**amp **sc**old **scr**ap	to**ld** e**lf** e**lk** ba**nk** cha**nce**
sled **sk**id **sl**ip	ba**nd** ba**ng** pa**nt** clea**nse** da**nce**
smut **sn**ip **sp**in **spl**at **spr**ing	ba**nk** ra**pt**
string **st**art **sw**ings	si**nk** gra**sp** fa**st**
trap **tr**ee **tw**in	sca**tch** ne**xt**

Exercises:

Read the blends in the tables in the page above and listen to the sounds they spell.

Read and write the words.

Activity: Beginning and ending consonant blends:

You can copy the following two pages.

Help your child to put the words together.

*Some **beginning** blends:*

***bl**ack **fr**og **pl**ant **sk**id **sl**ip **sn**ip **spr**ing*

*Some **ending** blends:*

*a**ct** ba**dge** le**ft** wa**lk** he**lp** ca**mp** ba**nk** ba**ng***

Match the beginning consonant blends with the word endings to make a word.

Beginning Consonant Blend	Vowel and Ending Consonant Blend
bl	*ant*
fr	*ip*
pl	*ap*
sk	*ing*
sl	*ack*
sn	*in*
spr	*ip*
sw	*ing*
tr	*og*
tw	*id*

Match the beginning of the word plus vowel with the final blend.

ba	*ct*
fa	*dge*
wa	*ft*
ca	*lk*
ba	*lp*
a	*mp*
ne	*nk*

le	*ng*
ba	*st*
he	*xt*

Lesson 12: Exercise: Read and Write these Words

Consonant Blends—Beginning—Final

Find and write ten beginning blends from the table.

Find and write ten final blends from the table.

nest	rest	mend	send
land	belt	bond	lend
just	pump	sulk	bulk
rust	hunt	hump	lump
jump	desk	mint	lamp
wept	sent	zest	must
band	fond	hint	dusk
bats	tops	camps	lisps
jumps	cups	pumps	melts
bran	clot	crab	drink
flat	frog	Glen	grab
print	scold	plant	skid
black	bran	clan	cram
act	drop	left	flat
frog	melt	glint	grab
Gwen	plant	print	scold
skid	scrap	shred	slid
smut	snip	spin	splat
sprint	start	string	swing

act	left	melt	bulb

Lesson 13: Long Vowel Sounds

The long vowel sounds sound the same as the letter names. The first letter of the vowel digraph names the sound. When a word has the vowel-consonant-final 'e' pattern, the final 'e' makes the vowel say its long sound. Examples, hat—hate pet—Pete pin—pine hop—hope cut—cute

/a-e/	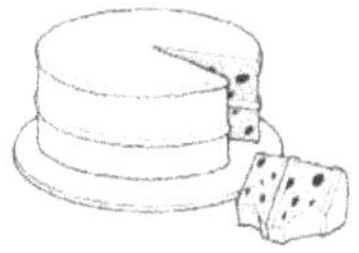	cake
/ee/		tree
/ie/		tie
/oe/	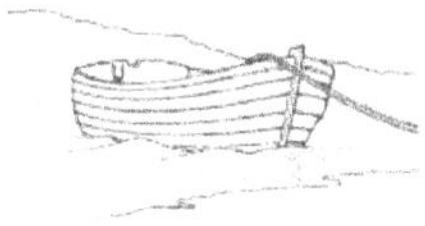	boat

/ue/	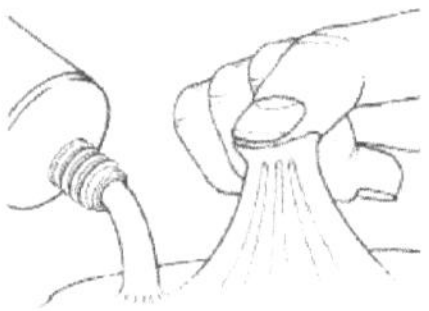	gl**ue**

Lesson 14: Long Vowel Sounds—Different Spelling

A **Digraph** is the name given to two letters when they are side by side in a word and used to spell one sound.

Remember: Long vowel sounds have more than one spelling. The different spellings are grouped for you to see.

Sound	Words
/ae/	l**a**k**e** r**ai**n pr**ay**
/ee/	**e**v**e** tr**ee** s**ea** sh**e** laz**y**
/ie/	k**i**nd d**ie** t**i**m**e** b**y** d**ye** b**uy** h**igh**
/oe/	g**o** t**oe** c**o**n**e** c**oa**t l**ow** th**ough** y**eo**man
/ue/	c**ue** c**u**t**e** f**ew** pn**eu**matic

Exercise: Help your child to find and write down five long vowel sounds in some words. Picture storybooks or a child's dictionary are helpful places to look for words.

Activity:

Read the sentences on the next page and write each underlined word. Note the spelling of the vowel sound/s in each word.

The **boat** was on the **lake.**

He left his **toy** in the **rain.**

Tom went to **church** to **pray.**

Eve saw a **movie** and had an **ice cream cone.**

The **bird** was sitting in the **tree.**

Many children have had a picnic by the **sea.**

She was having a **party** for her **birthday.**

Pedro, the donkey, was **very lazy.**

Her **teacher** was very **kind.**

The boy’s pet **snake** was going to **die.**

It is **time** to go and **eat tea.**

Although the **day** was, hot dad wore his **coat.**

We will **dye** the shirt **blue.**

The students went to **buy** some **sweets.**

The **plane** flew **high** in the **sky.**

Joe stubbed his **toe.**

Lesson 15: Vowel Sounds Spelled with Two Letters (Digraphs)

Digraph is the name given to two letters when they are side by side in a word to spell one sound.

These are **vowel digraphs**

Sound		Word
/oo/		moon
/oo/		book
/oy/		boy

/au/		(Santa) **Claus**
/aw/		**saw**
/ou/		**house**
/ow/		**owl**
/ow/	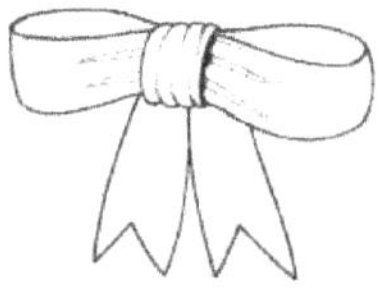	**bow**

Lesson 16: Double Vowel Rule

When two vowel sounds come together in the same word, you use the first vowel's long sound, and the second vowel is silent.

oat	bee	pay	say
ail	cue	eat	tie
day	been	due	way
aid	hay	fee	pie
beak	toad	deep	paid
goat	raid	leap	boat
neat	weak	keen	real
sail	heed	bean	rain
peep	road	heat	raid
float	fail	reap	lead
seam	weep	wail	week
seat	moat	peel	laid
peak	been	feel	gain
feet	deep	beam	maid
seed	jail	feet	need
gloat	fail	peat	lead
weak	neat	real	keen
seam	sleep	wail	peek
raid	heat	road	peep

Activity: Read and write these sentences.

It rained all week.

The road was wet from the rain.

The man paid for the coat.

The boat did not have a sail.

I will sail in the boat.

The deep moat was empty.

He paid to ride on the boat.

I need to go to feed the goat.

I eat tea each day.

The rain fell on the road.

Write some sentences of your own.

Add words with double vowels in them and read them out loud.

Lesson 17: The Other Vowel Sounds

The remaining eight vowel sounds are:

/air/	stair care where wear heir	/oo/ (long)	boot through do soup blue grew
/ar/	far pass palm	/oo/ (short)	Look put woman should
/er/	her bird fur word journey heard	/or/	for haul raw chalk ball board door pour bore war ought
/oi/	boil boy	/ow/	cow loud bough

EXERCISE: Read and write the sentences. Write some as well.

A man went up the stairs.

The boy did not go far from his house.

A bird was in the tree.

The boy and girl went to the fair.

The cow went moo as the boy went by.

The car made a loud bang.

The girl plays with a blue ball.

The bird sat on the bough of the tree.

Lesson 18: Consonant Sounds Spelled with Two Letters (Digraphs)

/ch/		**ch**icken
/ng/		ki**ng**
/qu/		**qu**een
/sh/		**sh**ip
/th/		**th**umb

Read and write the following words.

Write or underline the consonant digraphs in each word in colour. Write sentences using these words.

chicken	chip	chop	chant	chase	chisel
king	sing	wing	thing	bring	ding
queen	quit	quince	quiet	quest	quote
ship	shop	shut	dish	wish	sash
thumb	this	that	them	there	then

Lesson 19: Review of Vowels

Vowels

Different Spellings for Each Long Vowel Sound

<table>
<tr><td>/ae/</td><td colspan="2">ay tray say stay lay may
a-e cake make take wake lake grate
ai train rain gain brain drain main
ea great
eigh eight freight weight</td></tr>
<tr><td>/ee/</td><td colspan="2">e-e Pete Eve Steve
ee tree see been green
ea dream lean sea scream
e she we he me
y lazy happy silly</td></tr>
<tr><td>/ie/</td><td>i bind wind find
i-e kite bite ice spice
ye dye
igh high thigh</td><td>ie tie pie die
y cry try fly my
uy buyGuy</td></tr>
<tr><td>/oe/</td><td>o go no so
o-e bone cone tone
ow low below snow
eo yeoman</td><td>oe toe
oa coat boat moat
ough though although</td></tr>
<tr><td>/ue/</td><td>ue fuel cue
ew flew grew new
eu pneumatic pneumonia
u-e cute brute flute</td><td></td></tr>
</table>

Lesson 20: Consonant Digraphs with Alternate Spellings

Common Spelling		Alternate Spelling	
ch	/**ch**/ **ch**in	/**k**/ **ch**emist	/**sh**/ **ch**ef
ph	/**f**/ **ph**oto		
qu	/**qu**/ **qu**ack	/**k**/ **qu**iche	
sh	/**sh**/ **sh**ip		
th	/**th**/ unvoiced **th**ump	/**th**/ voiced **th**ere	
wh	/**wh**/ whack	/**h**/ **wh**om	
gh	/**f**/ lau**gh**	silent /**gh**/ hi**gh**	

Some other spellings:

'y' = **long /e/** sound - hungr**y** countr**y** fur**y**

'y' = **long /i/** sound - appl**y** den**y** magnif**y**

'ci' = **/sh/** sound - so**ci**al fa**ci**al ra**ci**al

'ti' = /**sh**/ sound - na**ti**on sta**ti**on

'ce' = **/sh/** sound – o**ce**an crusta**ce**an

'si' = /**zh**/ sound – vi**si**on divi**si**on

Lesson 21: Reading Practice

Read these sentences:

The duck went quack, quack.

Jill laughed out loud.

They all had quiche for tea.

The boy did not go far from his house.

The bird was in the tree.

The boy and girl went to the fair.

The cow went moo at the boy.

The car made a loud bang.

The girl plays with a blue ball.

She went to the shop today.

She paid for her ticket at the shop.

It is eight o'clock.

I see the tram at the tram-stop.

Bob left his key in the lock.

Bill got the bread from the shop.

Jill sat on the seat under the tree.

The bird sat on the bough of the tree.

Lesson 22: Syllables

A syllable is the smallest part of a word that has a vowel sound in it.

In English, we blend **25 consonant sounds** and **18 vowel sounds** into **syllables.**

Each English word has one or more of these fifteen syllable patterns: (**c** represents a consonant and **v** represents a vowel

CV = a consonant followed by a vowel)

CV, CCV, CCCV, CVC, CCVC, CCCVC, CVCC, CVCC, CCVCC, CCVCC, CCCVCCC, VCCC, VCC, VC, V

English has rules for words.

New words are invented all the time.

Their syllables must have one of the above patterns.

You can start working out the syllable patterns from the first vowel in a word.

Example: pic/nic is a two-syllable word. Each syllable has a **CVC** pattern. If a word has this pattern, you divide the syllables between the two consonants.

It can be easy to hear the syllables when you say the words.

A **Compound Word** contains two words.

seaweed	skateboard	newspaper	rainfall	snowflake
bathtub	workshop	homesick	eyesight	tradesman

Write out each compound word and then the two words that make it.

Lesson 23: Read and Write These Two-Syllable Words.

Read the words on the next page. The first syllable in each word ishighlighted.
Notice each syllable has a vowel sound.
If the word ends in **'y'** what vowel sound does it stand for?
Read each word to your child. Then ask them to say the word clapping each syllable. Example **ba** (clap) **ker** (clap) is **ba**ker
Write the words out in alphabetical order. If there is more than one word for a letter, look at the second and third letter to keep the alphabetical order.
Write out each word dividing them into syllables and highlighting the vowel sounds in colour. Example b**a**/k**er**

Read the words aloud and learn to spell these words.
Use a dictionary to check how each word is divided into syllables.

English Words Divided into Syllables (parts of a word containing a vowel sound)			
ba-ker	**a**-gain	**ne**-gro	**mid**-dle
gi-ant	**o**-ver	**se**-cret	**gra**-vy
cra-zy	**jel**-ly	**pa**-per	**si**-lent
hol-low	**ca**-per	**su**-gar	**pep**-per
cru-el	**hu**-man	**pi**-lot	**spi**-der
di-al	**i**-cy	**per**-son	**strum**-ming
di-et	**i**-dol	**po**-et	**strug**-gle
du-ty	**in**-side	**pre**-vent	**stu**-pid
ju-ry	**pen**-cil	**ta**-ken	**la**-dy

qui-et **tra**-der **sha**-dy **fa**-tal
fe-ver **la**-zy **re**-spect **tu**-tor
fi-nal **le**-gal **ri**-der **to**-tal
li-ar **ri**-ot **tri**-al **tru**-ant
flu-ent **li**-on **ru**-by **ru**-ler
fo-cus **ma**-ker **ru**-in **mut**-ter
fu-el **mo**-ment **ru**-ral **va**-cant
dan-ger **num**-ber **hap**-py **nut**-meg
vi-tal **din**-ner **nurs**-ing **dif**-fer
vo-cal **drum**-mer **hun**-dred **pam**-per
wa-fer **el**-der **hun**-ter **pa**-nel
wai-ter **em**-bers **in**-sect **pan**-try
en-ter **in**-to **pa**-tron **pat**-tern
fac-tor **jes**-ter **pen**-cil **em**-blem
ac-tor **ken**-nel **pen**-ny **fan**-cy

Reading Strategies

The first reading strategy to develop is an awareness of why an author writes a passage.

Authors write to:

- Persuade readers to accept their point of view
- To make the reader want to do something
- To give information
- To describe something
- To entertain their readers

Authors write to:

PERSUADE **INFORM** **DESCRIBE** **ENTERTAIN**

Comprehension involves understanding several strategies.

TWELVE READING STRATEGIES

1. Deciding on the **MAIN IDEA** the author is presenting.

   Teaching strategy: Ask:

   - What would be a good title?
   - What was this text/story about?

2. Point out the **FACTS** and **DETAILS**

   Teaching strategy: Ask pertinent questions. For example:

   - What did the second little pig use to build his house?
   - How many ducks went swimming in thepond?

3. Discuss the **ORDER** in which things happened in the text/story:
    - Who left home first?
    - When did the woodman come to grandma's house?

    Your child to become aware of the beginning, middle and end of stories and texts.

4. Noticing that something happens which affects what follows.

    CAUSE (why it happens) and **EFFECT (what happens).**
    - Building a house of straw made it easier for the wolf to blow it down.
    - It is hard for penguins to walk because their legs are short.

5. Noticing similarities and differences known as:

    COMPARING and CONTRASTING.

    For example:
    - The emu is a bird, but it cannot fly.
    - The other animals did not help little red hen.
    - How are the hare and tortoise alike?

6. **PREDICTING** what could happen next then checking if the author tells it the same way.

    For example:
    - Jack left his raincoat home. At lunchtime, it started to rain.

    PREDICTION:

    Jack will get wet, going home.

7. Using **CONTEXT** to work out the meaning of unknown words:

    For example:

    Jack had a nibble on his biscuit just as the bell rang. (Nibble = small bite)

    (The bell caused Jack to hurry!)

8. **INFERRING** from given information:

   For example:

   Jane put her hands over her ears when the train whistle blew.

   Inference: The whistle was loud and hurt her ears.

9. Knowing the difference between **FACT** and **OPINION**.

   For example:

   Mother baked some biscuits for the children. **FACT**

   Mother bakes yummy biscuits. **OPINION**

10. Assessing why the **AUTHOR WROTE** the text: Was it to?

    - persuade
    - inform
    - describe
    - entertain

    There can be more than one reason.

11. Recognizing **FIGURATIVE LANGUAGE** and knowing not to take it literally.

    For example:

    Bob said, "I'm not pulling your leg!" He means I am not tricking you. I am telling the truth.

12. Knowing the difference between **REAL and MAKE BELIEVE**.

    For example:

    Jack sat on the carpet, and suddenly it rose into the air. It could not happen without help. It is make-believe.

Examples of written forms are:

- short stories
- fables
- fairy stories

- poetry
- novels
- journal entries
- articles
- essays

There are two categories of **WRITTEN EXPRESSION**:

1. **FICTION** (NARRATIVE)
2. **NON FICTION**—INFORMATION

HOW TO PRESENT THE STORIES IN THIS BOOK

NEW STORY INTRODUCTION — This may occur over some sessions.

- Read each story through and have a thorough knowledge of it. Note anything you may have to explain or discuss with your child.

- Decide whether you need to give your child some background knowledge. Check the level of their experience.

- Note any words that need explaining before you begin reading.

- Introduce the story: give the **title** and a **short synopsis** or **summary**.

For example:

Ask: What do you think this story might be about? Have you heard this story before? Do you know a lot about wombats?

- Read the story with the child watching the text as you do so. Don't stop; read it all.

- Ask for the child's response. Ask some questions.

- Read the story together if your child is ready to do so.

- Ask your child to retell the story.

- Child reads the story. Encourage fluent reading by not interrupting. If they stumble over a word, just give it and review it later.

It is a good idea that your child writes about the story and illustrates his or her work.

Keep reading (daily) from the outstanding selection of children's books available.

Short Sentences

Read the sentences and then write them from memory

Sam has a dog.

Nan has a cat.

Sam gets a pet.

I met the pet.

The pig bit Sam.

The pig did a jig.

The pig got a big fig.

The sun is hot.

The hot dog sat on a log.

Sam and the dog jog.

Mick and Jack ran with the dog.

The bug was on the rug.

The bug had fun in the mug.

The dog and cat sat on the bigrug.

The big lad is mad at dad.

He paid to ride on the boat.

The following stories are to read and enjoy.
There are revision exercises included with some of the texts.
You can also write stories together and make them into a book to share.

Days to Play

What are the days a child can play?

Saturday, Sunday, Monday, Tuesday, Wednesday, Thursday, Friday, Saturday, Sunday, Monday.

Fishing

One, two, three, four, five,

Once I caught a fish alive.

Six, seven, eight, nine, ten

But I let it go again.

STORY 1

A Fat Rat

short vowel sound /**a**/

a

a rat a bat a man a cat

Pat bad

A rat sat on a mat.

A fat rat and a cat sat on a mat.

A bat sat on a mat.

A fat bat sat on a mat.

A bat and a cat sat on a mat.

A bad cat sat on a mat.

A cat, a rat and a bat sat on a mat.

Pat, in a hat, sat on a mat.

Can a man sit on a mat?

WORD DRILL: SOUND OUT & WRITE THE WORDS

c-at	b-at	f-at	h-at	at
m-at	r-at	s-at	P-at	an
a-nd	a-nt	c-an	f-an	m-an
p-an	r-an	v-an	c-ap	n-ap
t-ap	b-ag	r-ag	b-ad	gl-ad
h-ad	p-ad	s-ad	h-am	j-am

Draw

a cat
a bat
a hat
a mat
a man
a cap
a bag
a van

STORY 2

BEN AND THE HEN

short vowel sound /**e**/

Look and Say Words: **the** **was**

a hen
a pen
a nest
a shed

Meg
Ben

The red hen was in the nest.

The nest was in the pen.

An egg was in the nest.

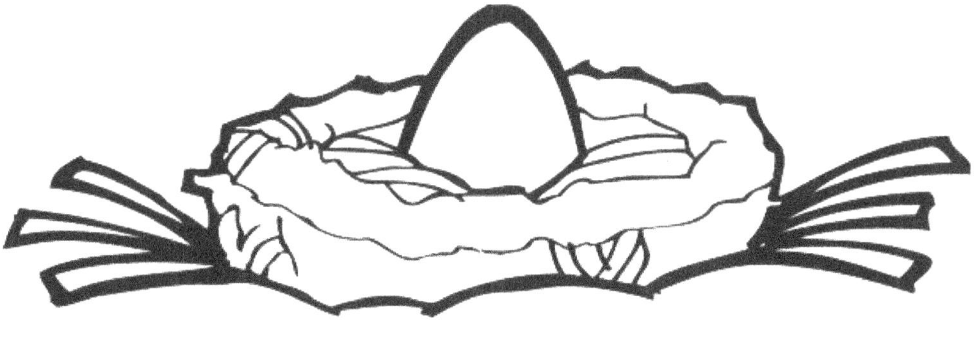

Meg went to the nest to get the egg.

Ben went in the shed to get the egg.

Red hen went to rest in the nest.

Meg and Ben let red hen rest in the nest.

WORD DRILL: SOUND OUT & WRITE THE WORDS

t-ell	p-eck	y-es	B-en	th-em
f-ell	d-eck	r-est	p-en	sh-elf
sm-ell	T-ed	n-est	h-en	h-elp
w-et	b-ed	b-est	wh-en	l-eft
g-et	b-eds	bl-ed	w-ent	st-ep
s-et	f-ed	w-ed	seven	cr-ept
s-ets	sh-ed	egg	th-en	n-ext
l-et	p-est	M-eg	ken-nel	tell
m-et	t-est	w-est	m-elt	p-elt

Draw: a hen; a nest; an egg; a shed; a pen; Ben; Meg

STORY 3

A BIG PIG

short vowel sound /**i**/

i

a pig

a kid a bin a wig

A big pig and a bin.

A kid sat on the lid of the bin.

Six kids and a pig did a jig on the bin.

A fat pig in a wig did a jig.

A big pig and a kid did a jig.

A fig is on the lid of the bin.

Can a pig in a wig sit on the bin?

WORD DRILL: SOUND OUT & WRITE THE WORDS

h-id	b-ig	b-in	n-ip	it
d-id	d-ig	d-in	d-ip	s-its
k-id	f-ig	s-in	s-ip	b-it
l-id	j-ig	w-in	lip	f-it
b-id	p-ig	f-in	p-ip	k-it
r-id	w-ig	t-in	r-ip	h-it
s-ix	f-ix	m-ix	sl-ip	p-it

Draw:

a fig; a pig; a bin; a lid; six kids; a kid;

a wig; a jig.

STORY 4

BOB AND TOM

short vowel sound /**o**/

Look and Say: **was** **the**

Bob frog Tom dog

Bob had a frog. Tom had a dog.

The frog sat in the pond.

Tom was hot. The dog was lost.

The dog was lost at the pond.

Tom went to the pond and got the dog.

Bob got a box for the frog. The frog got hot in the box.

Tom and Bob trot from the pond with the dog and the frog in the box.

WORD DRILL: SOUND OUT & WRITE THE WORDS

h-ot	b-og	p-ond	t-op	B-ob
n-ot	d-og	l-ong	p-op	c-ot
g-ot	fr-og	fr-om	m-op	on
p-ot	s-oft	T-om	h-op	d-ot
tr-ot	l-ost	b-ox	st-op	t-op
f-ox	p-ost	h-ost	fr-ost	pl-op

Draw

a dog

a pond

a lid

a frog

a box

Tom Bob

STORY 5

GUS AND THE PUP

short vowel sound /**u**/

u

Gus

a bug

a pup

a bun

Gus and the pup had fun in the sun.

The bug was on the mug.

Gus did not bump the mug.

But the pup did. The mug went in the mud.

The bug went on the cup and the bun.

Yum! Yum!

Gus and the pup went for a run in the hot sun.

The pup went in the mud and had lots of fun.

Gus must not jump in the mud with the pup.

No fun for Gus!

WORD DRILL: SOUND OUT & WRITE THE WORDS

up	d-ump	m-ud	b-ut	t-ug
p-up	h-ump	s-un	c-ut	b-ug
m-ust	p-ump	f-un	n-ut	l-ug
j-ust	r-ump	g-un	b-us	m-ug
j-ump	tr-unk	b-un	G-us	p-ug
b-ump	s-unk	n-un	us	y-um

Draw:

a pig, a bin, a lid, a pup, a kid, a wig, a jig, Gus.

The Game of Cricket

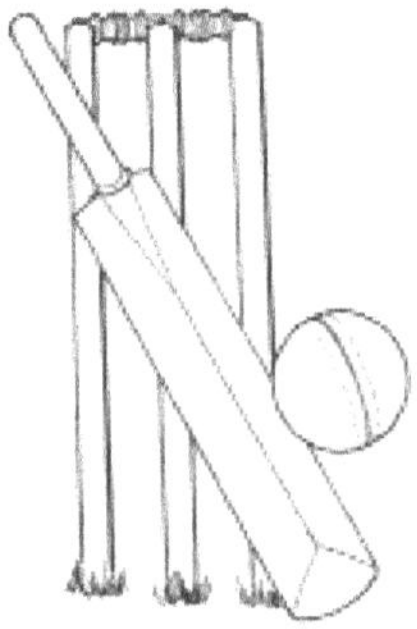

Dad gave Tom a cricket bat and ball. His mother gave him the stumps.

His friends, in his street, made a cricket pitch.

Then they played a game.

Ron batted and made seven runs.

He let the ball hit the stumps.

He was out. Tom batted next.

His second ball hit the wall.

Jim caught him out.

Jack was next to bat.

All the boys had fun.

The game went on till dark.

A Day at the Beach

The day was hot.

The family went to the beach.

Jan and John took a bucket and spade.

Mother took the picnic lunch.

Father put the beach umbrella in the car.

When they got to the beach, they went swimming.

Then the family had a picnic lunch.

Jan and John helped mother clear the picnic dishes.

Father put them back in the car.

Father bought them an ice-cream. Yum! Yum!

The family played cricket in the sand.

Then the children built a sandcastle.

The family left the beach at sunset.

On the way home, the children went to sleep in the car. Everyone had a happy day.

Planet Earth

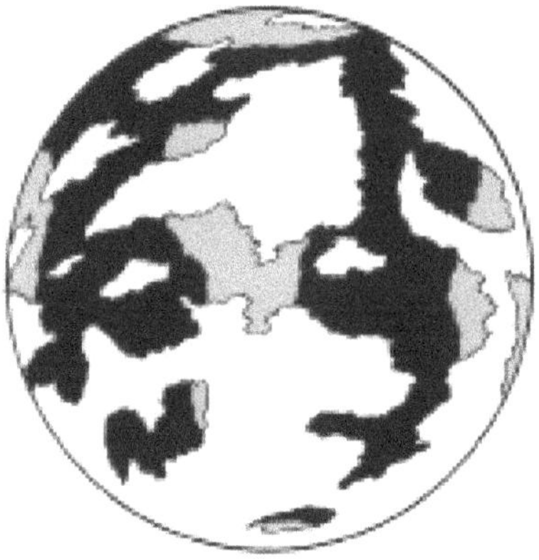

A planet goes around a star.

The sun is a star and has more than nine planets in its orbit.

Earth is the third planet from the sun.

Venus and Mars are the closest planets to Earth.

Rockets are sent from Earth to explore space.

Earth travels around the sun. It takes one year to do this.

Earth has the right amount of heat from the sun, and so life can live on Earth.

Plants and animals get warmth from the sun. Without the sun, all life on Earth would die.

Earth is also part of the Milky Way galaxy.

The Owl

What an odd bird an owl is.

An owl has big eyes to see in the dark.

It hunts at night.

An owl has excellent hearing.

Its claws are sharp, and its beak is like a hook.

Owls like to eat small creatures.

The owl is very quiet when it flies. Its wings do not make a noise at all.

Mice do not hear the owl coming until it is too late.

Owls do not build their nests like other birds.

They make their home in hollows of trees or holes in the ground. Some owls even take over the empty nests of other birds.

A baby owl is soft like a ball of wool with eyes in it.

There are over 100 kinds of owls.

The Wombat

The wombat is an Australian native animal.

There are three kinds of wombat:

1. The Common Wombat.
2. The Tasmanian Wombat.
3. The Hairy-nosed Wombat.

A grown wombat is about the size of a pig.

It has a fat thick-set body, short legs and sharp claws on the front paws to use to dig tunnels.

A wombat likes to stay in one home for life.

Wombats look for food at night and sleep all day.

Clever Ants

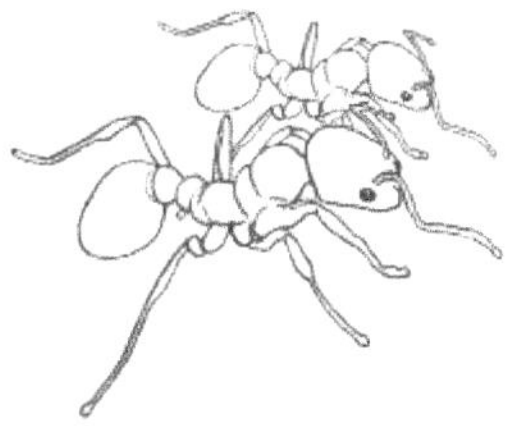

Ants work together in many ways.

They build colonies that are like little cities.

Ants are hard workers. They work together to hunt for food.

Large groups of ants can attack a large animal such as a snake and kill it.

Thousands of wingless worker ants, queen ant and drones live in an ant colony.

The workers look after the drones and queen.

A queen ant can live for fifteen years.

Queen ants have the babies for their colony.

Worker ants can live for seven years or longer.

Traditional Stories for Reading Pleasure

THE LITTLE RED HEN

A Traditional Story

Little Red Hen found a grain of wheat.

She said, "Who will take the wheat to the mill?"

"Not me," said the dog. "Not me," said the cat. "Not me," said the duck. "Not me," said the rat.

"I will take it myself," said the Little Red Hen.

Little Red Hen took the grain to it to the mill. The wheat was ground into flour.

"Who will bake bread with this flour?" said the Little Red Hen.

"Not me," said the dog. "Not me," said the cat.

"Not me," said the duck. "Not me," said the rat.

"Then I will bake it myself," said the Little Red Hen.

She made the bread and baked it.

"Who will eat the bread?"

said the Little Red Hen.

"I will," said the dog. "I will," said the cat.

"I will," said the duck. "I will," said the rat.

"No! I will eat it myself," said the Little Red Hen.

And she called her chickens to help her.

THE LION AND THE MOUSE

Adapted from an Aesop Fable

A lion was sleeping in the sun when a little mouse ran over his nose and woke him up.

The lion was going to kill the little mouse when she said, "Do not kill me. One day I might help you."

The lion let the mouse go, and she ran to her nest.

The next day the lion was caught in a trap made from rope. He couldn't get out.

"Oh, dear," said the lion. "How can I get free?"

"I will set you free," said the little mouse.

She stopped running and started to chew the ropes one by one with her sharp teeth, till the lion was free.

"Thank you, little mouse," said the lion. "I am glad I set you free."

THE ANT AND THE GRASSHOPPER

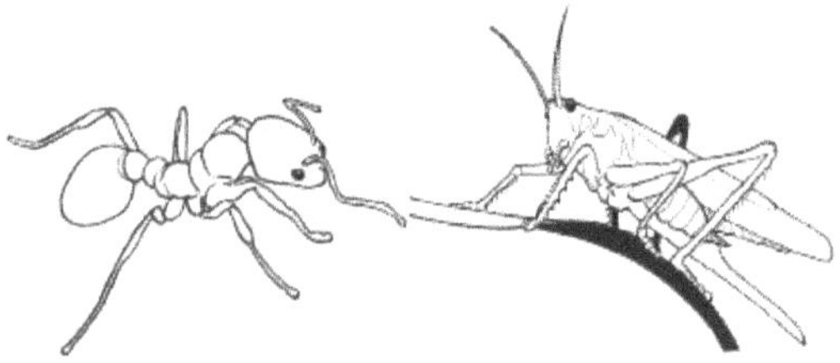

Adapted from an Aesop Fable

One sunny autumn day, an ant was busy storing food for winter.

A grasshopper was sitting on a log nearby enjoying the sunshine and watching her work.

"Why are you so busy on such a lovely day?" he asked.

"I will have food for winter," she replied. "Will you?"

"It is too sunny for work!" said the grasshopper.

The ant went on working, and the grasshopper kept resting.

The winter that year was freezing.

The grasshopper was starving.

He asked the ant for food. She had none to spare.

The grasshopper went away, feeling scared.

He was sorry he had not prepared for winter.

Lesson: We need to prepare for future needs.

THE DONKEY AND THE SALT

Retold from an Aesop Fable

A man took his donkey to get a load of salt.

On the way home, he had to cross the river. The donkey slipped on a stone in the river and fell into the water. The wet salt melted, and there was none left.

The load was light, and the lazy donkey was happy.

The donkey thought,

"That was a good trick. I will do it again."

The next day, the man put a load of sponges on the donkey's back. When they came to the river, the donkey fell to make his burden light.

The sponges were heavy when full of water.

The donkey could barely walk with such a heavy load.

The next day he crossed the river and did not fall.

Lesson: Luck won't always be on your side.

THE SUN AND THE WIND

Adapted from an Aesop Fable

"I am stronger than you," said the wind to the sun.

"I can turn a windmill. You cannot do that."

The sun said, "I cannot turn a windmill, but I am stronger than you. I can make the flowers open and ripen the corn."

Just then, a man came along. He wore a long coat.

"I will show you that I am stronger than you," said the wind. "I will blow the man's coat off." He blew and blew, but he could not blow the coat off.

"It is my turn now," said the sun. It shone brightly and made the man feel hot. The sun kept on shining until the man felt too hot and took off his coat.

"Yes," said the wind. "You must be stronger than I, for you have done what I could not do."

Lesson: Kindness and persuasion win over force.

THE BOY WHO CRIED WOLF

Adapted from an Aesop Fable

There was once a shepherd-boy who looked after a flock of sheep on a hill outside the village.

One day he thought he would have some fun and trick the villagers. So he began to cry and ran toward the village.

"Wolf! Wolf! Come and help! The wolves are taking my lambs!" he yelled.

The villagers stopped working and ran to the hill to help him save the lambs.

When the villagers reached the sheep, the boy laughed at them. He said, "I was only joking. There was no wolf there!"

The villagers went back to the village. They were angry with the shepherd-boy.

On another day, the shepherd-boy tried the same trick.

When the villagers came running to help, he laughed at them again.

However, one day, a wolf appeared and began killing the lambs. The terrified boy ran for help.

"Wolf! Wolf!" he screamed. "There is a wolf in the flock! Help! Help!" The villagers heard the boy but thought it was another trick.

They kept on working. No one went to help.

That time the shepherd-boy lost all his sheep.

LESSON: If you lie, there can come a time when no one believes you.

THE HARE AND THE TORTOISE

Retold from an Aesop Fable

One day a hare, who ran as fast as the wind, was laughing at the slow, old tortoise. "What short legs you have," he said scornfully.

"Even though you are as swift as the wind, I will beat you in a race," the tortoise said.

The hare thought this was impossible and agreed to a race.

"I simply can't lose," the hare said to himself.

The fox chose the course and fixed the winning post.

As they walked up to the starting line, the hare was running around in circles and teasing the tortoise. The tortoise said nothing and lined up behind the line, ready for the race to begin.

"Ready, set, go!" called the fox.

The hare was up the first hill before the tortoise had reached the first bend in the road. But the tortoise kept plodding along, his eye on the way. He never stopped.

The hare got a long way ahead of the tortoise. He decided to take a break until the tortoise caught up.

The sun was warm, and the hare fell fast asleep.

The tortoise kept plodding on and passed the hare.

At last, the hare woke up only to see the tortoise cross the finishing line.

Lesson: Slow and steady wins the race.

THE THREE LITTLE PIGS

A Traditional Story

Once upon a time, there lived three little pigs.

One day they left their mother to build homes of their own.

The first little pig built a house of straw.

The big, bad wolf came by the straw house. "Let me come in," he said.

"Not by the hair of my chinny, chin, chin," said the little pig. "I will not let you in. “Then I will huff, and I will puff. I will blow your house in," said the big, bad wolf.

He blew the straw house down.

The little pig ran as fast as he could to the second little pig's home.

The second little pig had a house of sticks.

He let his brother into his house. Soon the big, bad wolf came to the stick house. "Let me come in," the wolf said to the two little pigs.

"Not by the hair of our chinny, chin, chins," said the two little pigs. "We will not let you in."

"I will huff, and I will puff. I will blow your house in," said the big, bad wolf.

He blew the stick house down. The two little pigs ran as fast as they could to the third little pig's house.

The third little pig had a brick house.

The three little pigs were in the brick house when the big, bad wolf knocked on the door. "Let me come in," he said.

"Not by the hair of our chinny, chin, chins," said the three little pigs. "We will not let you in."

"Then I will huff, and I will puff. I will blow your house in," said the big, bad wolf.

The wolf huffed and puffed. He could not blow the brick house down.

The wolf climbed onto the roof of the brick house.

He was going to drop down the chimney and grab the three little pigs. He did not know there was a large pot of boiling water on the fire.

The wolf slid down the chimney and fell splash into the pot of boiling water. He screamed and ran from the house.

The wolf never came that way again.

The three little pigs lived happily ever after, in the safe, small brick house.

THE GREAT BIG TURNIP

Retold from the Story by Alexi Tolstoy

A man, his wife and a little boy lived in the country.

One day the man planted some turnip seeds. Soon little turnip leaves poked up through the brown soil.

The next day, the little boy, saw one turnip plant was growing faster than the rest. It kept on growing and growing.

"We will have turnip soup tonight," said the man.

He went to pull the turnip out of the ground, but it was stuck.

He called his wife, "Come and help me pull out the turnip. It is stuck."

The man and his wife pulled and pulled, but they could not remove the turnip out of the ground.

"Son, son," called the woman to the little boy, "Come and help us pull the turnip out of the ground."

The little boy came running over and put his arms around his mother's waist. She had her arms around the man's waist. They pulled and pulled and pulled and pulled. But the turnip stuck fast. The boy called the dog, who then pulled the boy. The turnip still held fast. The hen came next, and she pulled the dog.

But the turnip still stuck fast.

"Cluck, cluck, cluck," the hen called to the rooster.

The man, the woman, the boy, the dog, the hen and now the rooster all pulled on the turnip.

They pulled and pulled and pulled.

Suddenly with a 'whoosh', the turnip came out of the ground.

Everyone tumbled into a heap and started to laugh.

The dog, hen and rooster did too. No-one was hurt.

The man, woman and little boy rolled the enormous turnip into their house. The wife cooked it for dinner.

Everyone had plenty to eat.

There was enough left for lunch the next day and the next and the day after that.

A STONE IN THE ROAD

Retold from a Classic Oriental Fairy Tale

Long ago, there was a town where the men did not want to work.

The rich man did not like this.

One day he put a large stone in the middle of the road. Every day, the lazy townsmen walked along the road. They saw the stone in the way, but no one went to move it.

One sunny day, a boy came walking along the road.

He saw the large stone. He thought, "I must move that stone before someone trips over it."

The massive stone was hard to move. The boy pushed the boulder, for a long time, until finally, he was able to move it, to the side of the road.

Then the boy saw a large bag in the middle of the road. It had been under the stone. He opened it and saw it was full of gold coins.

Soon the rich man came along and said to the boy: "I put the bag under the stone. The gold coins were for the person who moved the stone from the middle of the road."

"You are the only one in the town who was not too lazy to move the stone," the rich man told the boy.

"The gold coins are yours for you earned them."

The boy could not believe his luck and ran home with his fortune.

THE TOWN MOUSE AND COUNTRY MOUSE

Retold from an Aesop Fable

A town mouse went to visit his country cousin.

The country mouse tried to give the town mouse an enjoyable time.

The town mouse did not enjoy the holiday in the country.

"How can you live, in this little hole, in the barnyard? It is so small and dark," the town mouse said to the country mouse.

"Come with me to the city, and you can stay in the fine house I live in," said the town mouse to the country mouse.

The town mouse did not like the food the country mouse gave him either.

"Come to my house, and I will show you the best food in the world," said the town mouse as he left to go home.

One day, the country mouse went to see the town mouse.

He reached the townhouse safely and settled in.
The country mouse felt comfortable sitting on a luxurious carpet and eating scraps of all kinds of leftover food from dinner. The food was tasty.
The country mouse enjoyed himself and did not miss his home at all. Suddenly the door opened, and in ran three large barking dogs.
The country mouse was frightened.
He ran from the house before the dogs saw him.
He had a lucky escape. He scampered to his tiny country home.
When he got home and caught his breath, he thought, "Town life is not for me. I would rather live safely in my poor little hole than in a fine townhouse where I am not safe."

Lesson:

Don't envy rich people for they often have many troubles.

KING MIDAS

Adapted from the Greek Myth: Midas and the Golden Touch

Once upon a time, there lived a king named Midas. He lived in a beautiful palace with his young daughter, whom he truly loved.

King Midas was a rich man who always wanted more gold.

One day, a fairy came to him and said, "You may have one wish."

"I wish for lots more gold," said the King. "I wish that everything I touch turns into gold."

" You shall have your wish, but it will not make you happy," said the fairy.

When King Midas woke the next morning, his bed had turned to gold. He got out of bed and touched a chair. That turned to gold too.

He put on his clothes, and they turned to gold.

During his morning walk, every flower he touched became a golden flower. "How happy I am!" he thought.

King Midas sat down to breakfast. He could not eat. As he touched his food, it turned into gold.

His daughter, who had been in the garden, ran in and kissed him. As soon as her lips touched her father, she turned into gold.

King Midas felt sad, for he loved his daughter.

Now he could eat no food, and he had lost his dear little daughter.

Suddenly he looked up and saw the fairy standing near.

"Are you happy now, King Midas?" said the fairy. "No, no, no!" cried the King. "Give me back my little daughter. I do not want gold anymore."

"Then go down to the river and jump in. The golden touch will leave you," said the fairy. "Throw some water over your little girl so she can come back to you."

The fairy flew away.

King Midas ran down to the stream. He jumped in.

He filled a jug with water and threw it over his little girl. She came to life and ran and kissed him.

This time she did not turn to gold, for the golden touch had left King Midas forever.

King Midas learned that having gold doesn't always make you happy.

THE TORTOISE THAT TALKED TOO MUCH

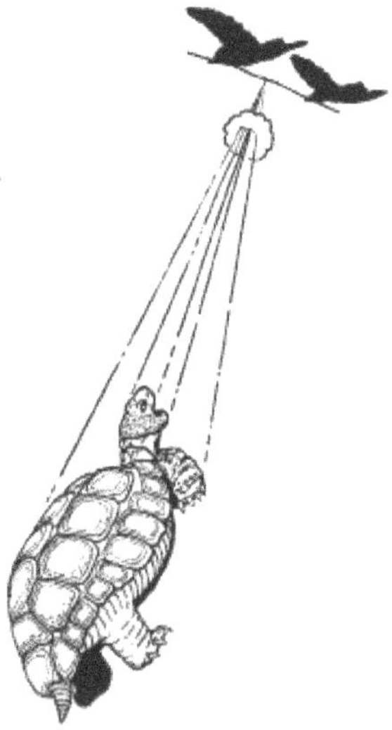

An Indian Fable from the Panchatantra

Tortoise and two ducks lived in a pond. They were friends.

Now Tortoise loved to talk. She was always talking.

One year the pond dried up. The ducks knew they would have to go to another one.

They said goodbye to the Tortoise.

"Oh, do not leave me behind!" she begged. "Please take me!"

"But you cannot fly," said the ducks.

"How can we take you with us?"

"Leave me behind, and I will die," wailed Tortoise.

The ducks felt sorry for little Tortoise.

They thought about how Tortoise could go with them.

They had an idea.

"Each of us will take hold of one end of a big, fat stick. You can bite the middle. We will fly up in the air together.

"You must not talk or open your mouth. If you do, you will fall to the ground," the ducks said.

Tortoise promised not to speak.

The ducks and Tortoise rose into the air and started to fly.

Tortoise kept her mouth shut until they flew over a village.

The people laughed to see such a sight.

"Do not be so rude!" said Tortoise.

Because Tortoise had opened her mouth to speak, she fell right to the ground.

The ducks were so sorry to lose their young friend.

LESSON:

At times, it can be better to hold one's tongue.

THE SPIDER AND THE FLY

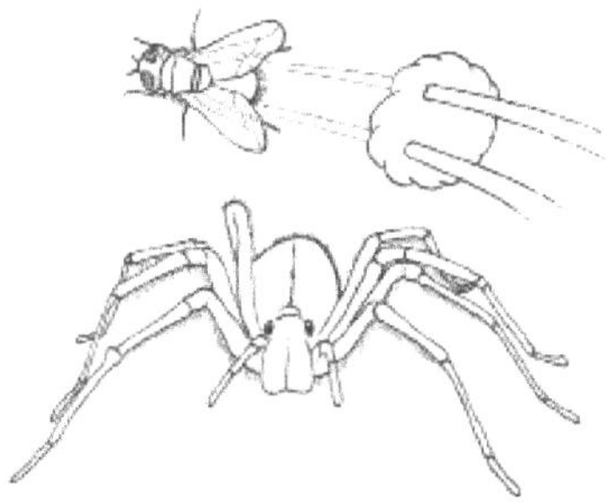

Based on the Poem 'The Spider and the Fly' by Mary Howitt (1799-1888)

Spider was big and fat around the middle.

He wore a dark brown coat and brown socks on eight legs.

One day he was sitting in his web, crying. Every time a tear fell from his eye, it fell on his web.

He cried fast, and as he had eight eyes, the web was soon shining in the sun.

Fly came flying past.

"Why do you cry Spider?" she asked. "I am so lonely," said Spider. Eight tears fell from his eight eyes.

"I wish I could help you," said kind Fly. Spider dried one eye.

"So you can," he said.

"How?" asked Fly.

Spider dried two eyes. "You can sit by my side," he said.

"Oh," said Fly. I cannot do that."

"Why not?" asked Spider. "I like flies."

"I know you do, and that is why I shall not come," said Fly.

Spider looked at her, and she saw his eight cunning eyes.

Fly flew round and round in the sun.

"Do not do that," Spider cried. "You make me feel giddy."

Fly came back and saw Spider was talking to himself.

He did not know that Fly could hear him.

He was saying, "A fine fat Fly, fried in butter."

"You horrid Spider," cried Fly.

Round and round she flew, round and round and round.

Spider grew so dizzy that he fell off his web into a pool of water.

Fly was safe.

LITTLE RED RIDING HOOD

Retold Story by The Brothers Grimm

Once there lived a little girl who had a beautiful red cloak with a hood. She wore it all the time. Everyone called her Little Red Riding Hood.

One day her mother said, "I want you to take a basket of cakes to your grandmother. She is not well."

Little Red Riding Hood put on her red cloak. As she was leaving, her mother said, "Go straight to Grandma's house through the woods, and do not talk to anyone."

On the way, she met a wolf. "Good morning Little Red Riding Hood. Where are you going this fine morning?" said the wolf smiling wickedly.

"I am taking cakes to my sick grandmother," said Little Red Riding Hood.

"Where does your Grandma live?" asked the wolf.

"In a cottage at the edge of the wood," said Little Red Riding Hood.

The wolf was hungry and wanted to eat Little Red Riding Hood. He heard a woodcutter coming and ran away as fast as he could to Grandma's house.

He got inside and ate Grandma up in one gulp.

He dressed in Grandma's bedclothes and jumped into her bed just in time. He snuggled down into the bedclothes waiting for Little Red Riding Hood.

She knocked at the door.

"Come in!" said the wolf in a low voice. Little Red Riding Hood went over to the bed.

"What big eyes you have Grandma," she said.

"So I can see you clearly," replied the wolf.

"What big ears you have Grandma," said Little Red Riding Hood. "So I can hear you clearly," said the wolf.

Little Red Riding Hood saw the wolf's big nose and mouth. She wanted to scream. Instead, she said," What a big mouth you have Grandma."

"So I can eat you up," cried the wolf. He jumped out of bed and ate her up.

At that moment, the woodcutter was passing by the house.
He saw the door was open, so he went inside.
The woodcutter saw the wolf. He rushed at him and cut off his head with his sharp axe.
Grandma and Little Red Riding Hood jumped out. They were safe.
Little Red Riding Hood thanked the woodcutter and ran home.
She never ran alone through the woods again.

THE THREE BILLY GOATS GRUFF

Retold from a Norwegian Folktale

There were three billy goats named Gruff.

One day they went to the hillside to make themselves fat.

On the way, they had to cross the bridge over the river.

Underneath the bridge lived an ugly troll.

The troll had eyes as wide as saucers and a nose as long as a poker. The youngest Billy Goat Gruff went over the bridge first.

The bridge went trip, trap, trip.

The troll roared, "Who's that tripping over my bridge?"

"It is I, the youngest Billy Goat Gruff. "I am going to the hillside to make myself fat."

"No, you're not!" roared the troll. "I'm coming to gobble you up."

"Don't take me," said the youngest Billy Goat Gruff. "I am too little. Second Billy Goat Gruff comes next. He is much bigger than me."

"Well, move on," said the troll.

Soon the second Billy Goat Gruff came to the bridge. The bridge went trip, trap, trip.

The troll roared, "Who's that tripping over my bridge?"

"It is me," said second Billy Goat Gruff. "I'm going to the hillside to make myself fat."

"No, you're not!" roared the troll. "I'm coming to gobble you up."

"Don't take me," said the second Billy Goat Gruff. "Wait a bit until the third Billy Goat Gruff comes. He is much bigger than me."

"Well, move on," said the troll.

Then along came mighty Billy Goat Gruff. The bridge went trip, trap, trip.

Big Billy Goat Gruff was powerful. The bridge creaked and groaned as he moved across it.

The troll roared, "Who's that tramping over my bridge?"

"It's me! Big Billy Goat Gruff." He had a loud, ugly voice.

"I'm coming up to gobble you up," roared the troll.

"Well, come along!" challenged Big Billy Goat Gruff.

"I've got two spears to poke your eyeballs out at your ears. I've got two curling-stones to crush you to bits, body and bones." said the angry Big Billy Goat Gruff.

Big Billy Goat Gruff ran at the troll. He poked his eyes out with his horns. He then crushed his body and threw him into the river.

Big Billy Goat Gruff strolled across the bridge to meet his brothers on the hillside.

They ate so much grass they could barely walk home.

THE UGLY DUCKLING

Retold from a story by Hans Christian Andersen

Once upon a time, down on a farm, Mother Duck was sitting on six eggs. One bright morning the eggs hatched and out popped six ducklings.

Mother Duck looked again and saw the big seventh egg.

A pecking sound was coming from it. "How did it get there?" thought Mother Duck.

An ugly duckling, with grey feathers, came out of the egg.

"This duckling cannot be mine," she thought.

"He is not pretty like his brothers and sisters. He is much bigger too."

As the days passed the Ugly Duckling became more and more miserable. His brothers and sisters did not want to play with him. The farmyard animals laughed at him.

Mother Duck did her best to look after him. "Sad little Ugly Duckling!" she would say.

"Nobody loves me," he said each night as he cried himself to sleep.

One day he ran away from home. He asked everyone he met, "Do you know any ducklings with grey feathers like mine?"

No-one did. Everyone thought he was the ugliest duckling they had ever seen.

One day a countrywoman, thinking he was a lost goose, caught the Ugly Duckling and locked him up in a pen.

He did not know what to do.

One night, the countrywoman, forgot to lock the pen. The Ugly Duckling escaped.

He found a clump of reeds near a pond and decided to hide.

"I will hide here forever. There is plenty to eat," he thought.

One day at sunrise, he looked up into the sky. He saw a flock of beautiful birds flying overhead. They were white, with long, slender necks, yellow beaks and large wings. They were flying south.

"I wish I could go with them," he thought.

The winter was cold.

The Ugly Duckling could not find any food and lay exhausted on the ground.

A farmer found him and put him in his coat pocket. He took him home to his children. "They will look after him," he thought.

The Ugly Duckling lived in the warmth of the farmer's home for the rest of winter.

When spring came, the Ugly Duckling had grown. The farmer set him free by the pond.

That was when he saw himself in the water.

"I have changed," he thought. "I am not an Ugly Duckling anymore."

He had turned into a swan.

The flock of birds had returned from the south.

"You are one of us," they said.

As the young swan swam with his new family, a child said, "Look at that young swan. He is the finest of them all."

The young swan's heart almost burst with joy.

He was happy at last.

HOW THE DROUGHT WAS BROKEN

A Story Based on the Dream-time Stories of the Australian Aboriginal People

Once upon a time, the rivers and creeks in Australia dried out. The animals and the birds were extremely thirsty.

They called a meeting to see what they could do. The kookaburra sat in a gum-tree, laughing out loud.

"Ha-ha, hoo-hoo, ha-ha, hoo-hoo, there is no water to drink, not one drop" he sang.

A large crow flew to the gum-tree and sat on a branch.

The little koala in the tree asked, "Can you tell us where the water has gone?"

"A huge frog has drunk all the waters of Australia," said the wise old crow.

"What can we do?" said emu.

"We must make the frog laugh so he will open his mouth and let all the water out," said the crow.

"An excellent plan," said the kangaroo. "Take us to the huge frog."

The enormous crow led all the birds and animals to a vast cave. In front of it sat the biggest frog in the world.

The frog looked at all the birds and animals blinking his eyes.

The kookaburra was the first to try to get the frog to laugh.

The kookaburra laughed, "Ha-ha, hoo-hoo, ha-ha, hoo-hoo."

The huge frog looked at him but did not smile. The cranes danced next. Everyone, except the frog, thought their dance was funny. The huge frog almost fell asleep.

Little koala tried to make the frog laugh, by turning head over heels and letting other animals play football with him. The frog took a quick look and shut his eyes again.

Then it was the kangaroo's turn.

Kangaroo jumped and twisted and waved his paws.

The frog still did not smile and sat there, holding all the waters of Australia inside.

Every bird and animal, except the eel, had tried. No one had made the frog laugh.

"Let me try," said the eel.

"You!" screamed the parrots. "You are not at all funny!"

"I may as well try," said the eel. "There is no one else who can make the frog laugh."

"Yes, you must try!" said all the birds and animals together. "If you cannot make the frog laugh, we will all die of thirst."

The eel, looking solemn, began to dance on the tip of his tail.
The huge frog opened his eyes and looked at the eel.
He began to smile.
The eel kept dancing and looking very serious.
The frog began to laugh and opened his mouth as wide as could be.
All the waters of Australia rushed out of his enormous mouth.
They filled the rivers, lakes and creeks.
The kookaburra, the emu, the cranes, kangaroo, little koala and wise old crow all had a long, long drink. All the other birds and animals did too.
"Ha-ha, hoo-hoo, ha-ha, hoo-hoo," laughed kookaburra,
"I am amusing, but the eel is funnier than I am."
All the birds and animals agreed.

THE TAR BABY

Adapted from Uncle Remus Folktales

Mr Rabbit liked to tease Mr Fox. Mr Fox tried to catch Mr Rabbit.

One day Mr Fox said, "I must catch that rude rabbit."

Mr Fox made a tar baby from sticky tar. It had a tar head and a tar body. It had tar legs and tar arms too.

"I shall catch Mr Rabbit now," said Mr Fox. He put the tar baby on the side of the road.

Then Mr Fox hid in the bushes.

Soon Mr Rabbit came down the road. He saw the tar baby smiling at him. "Good morning," said Mr Rabbit to the tar baby.

The tar baby did not speak. He just kept on smiling. Mr Fox still hid in the bushes.

Mr Rabbit again said, "Good morning."

The tar baby did not speak. He kept on smiling. "Can't you

speak?" said Mr Rabbit.

The tar baby did not speak. Mr Fox still hid in the bushes.

"I'll make you speak," said Mr Rabbit. He hit the tar baby with his fist.

His fist stuck to the sticky tar baby.

"Let me go," said Mr Rabbit, "or I'll hit you again." The tar baby did not speak.

Mr Fox still hid in the bushes.

Then Mr Rabbit hit the tar baby with his other fist. That stuck too. "Let me go, or I will kick you!" yelled Mr Rabbit.

The tar baby still did not speak. Mr Fox still hid in the bushes.

Then Mr Rabbit kicked the tar baby with his foot. His foot stuck. He kicked it with his other foot, and it stuck too. Then he butted the tar baby with his head. His head stuck.

Mr Rabbit was stuck to the tar baby. He could not move. Mr Fox came out from the bushes.

"Ha! Ha!" said Mr Fox. "At last, I have caught you, Little Mr Rabbit. You will not get away now. "

"Mr Fox, please let me go. I will not tease you again," said Mr Rabbit.

"No," said Mr Fox. "I think I will make a fire and burn you up."

"Very well," said Mr Rabbit. "Burn me if you like, but please — please, Mr Fox, do not throw me into the bushes."

"No, I will not burn you," said Mr Fox. "I think I will throw you in the river."

"Drown me if you like, but please — please Mr Fox do not throw me into the bushes."

Because Mr Fox wished to harm Mr Rabbit, he said, "That is just what I will do."

He took hold of Mr Rabbit's hind legs and threw him right into the bushes.

"Thank you, Mr Fox," said Mr Rabbit. "That was just what I wanted."

He laughed out loud as he ran to his burrow in the bushes.

THE GINGERBREAD BOY

Retold from a Traditional Folk Story

Once upon a time, there lived a man, a woman and a little boy.

One morning, the woman made some gingerbread. She cut out a Gingerbread Boy. Then she placed him in the oven to bake.

"Little boy," she said, "I am going into the garden. Watch the oven. When the Gingerbread Boy is ready, let me know."

Soon the little boy heard a popping noise.

The oven door opened and out jumped the Gingerbread Boy. He ran across the kitchen and out the door.

The little boy followed the Gingerbread Boy, who was running away. The little boy called the woman and the man. He told them to chase the Gingerbread Boy.

The Gingerbread Boy was running too fast. No one could catch him.

When they stopped to rest, the Gingerbread Boy ran on, leaving them behind.

Still running the Gingerbread Boy came across two men who were digging by the road.

"Where are you going Gingerbread Boy?" called the men.

The Gingerbread Boy laughed and said," I have outrun the little boy, the woman and the man. I can beat you!"

"We'll see about that!" said the men. They started to chase him.

Although they ran fast, the men could not catch the Gingerbread Boy. On and on, he ran.

By and by, he came to a big bear. The bear asked, "Where are you going Gingerbread Boy?" The Gingerbread Boy shouted, "I've outrun a man, a little boy, a woman, and two road workers. I can outrun you!"

"We'll see about that!" growled the bear.

The bear trotted along, after the Gingerbread Boy. The bear was left behind as well.

On and on ran the Gingerbread Boy. By and by, he saw a fox. The sly fox was lying in a field. "Where are you going, Gingerbread Boy?" asked the fox.

The Gingerbread Boy shouted," I've run faster than the man, the little boy, the woman, two road workers, and the big bear. I can run faster than you!"

"We'll see about that!" thought the fox with a grin.
The fox said, "I can't hear you, Gingerbread Boy. Please come a little closer." Curious, the Gingerbread Boy, stopped running. He went close to the fox.
He said, "The man, the little boy, the woman, two road workers, and the big bear couldn't catch me. I can run faster than you too! You won't catch me!"
The fox grabbed him and said, "You can, can you?"
As the fox started to eat him, the Gingerbread Boy said," Oh dear! He has eaten a quarter of me.
Then in a tiny voice said, Oh, I'm half gone."
And then in a wee, little voice said, "I'm almost gone."
Finally, in a tiny, tiny, small voice, the Gingerbread Boy squeaked, "I'm all gone." The fox licked his lips and grinned.

That was the sad end of the Gingerbread Boy.

APPENDIX

Reading Behaviour Check List One		
Does your child:	**Yes**	**Not Yet**
Listen and concentrate when you read to him or her.		
Look at and attempt to read books chosen from a variety of sources. (for example own books, family books, library		
Ask family members to share his or her books with him/her.		
Attempt to read aloud from self-chosen books.		
Know the difference between fiction and nonfiction texts.		
Attempt to write and share their writing and illustrations.		
Recognize familiar logos and know for what they stand. (For example, Apple Logo, Kmart and Office Works).		
Print their name and recognize their name in print.		
Use visual cues to read and follow instructions.		
Comment on films, television programs, advertisements and DVDs.		
Know what an author does.		
Know what an illustrator does.		
Understand the sequence of stories and predict what could come next.		
Understand that the words and message in a written text don't change.		
Concentrate on the meaning in a story and not individual words.		
Comment about plot, characters and setting of a story.		
Recognize some words in a printed text.		

Recognize some words on posters, in advertisements, icons on a computer.		
Know the beginning and end of texts read or viewed.		
Recognize some high-frequency words such as 'the' 'and' 'Mother' 'Father'.		
Look for and find familiar words and letters in texts.		
Read text from left to right, top to bottom.		
Know the difference between print and pictures.		
Identify the title of a book or CD.		
Locate front and back cover of a book, cassette or video.		
Recognize that letters or characters make up words.		
Recognizes common symbols on acomputer screen or keyboard.		
Use some computer software and online resources.		
Understand that a sentence is made up of words and that they are separated by spaces.		
Have some letter/sound knowledge.		
Recognize letters, words, numbers and punctuation in simple texts.		
Notice and respond to punctuation in text and own writing.		

Reading Behaviour Check List Two		
Does your child:	**Yes**	**Not Yet**
Understand reading is a part of everyday life.		
Read aloud to you with confidence. Read fluently.		
Recognizefictionandnonfictionbooksandreadboth types.		
Share his or her written pieces with others.		
Read signs and brand names in everyday situations.		
Read simple instructions.		
Retell main ideas from television programs, advertisements and films.		
Understand the role of an author.		
Understand the role of an illustrator.		
Comment about what he/she reads.		
Discuss characters and setting of written and visual texts.		
Sees a relationshipbetweenwhatis readandtheir experience.		
Have a growing written and spoken vocabulary.		
Comment on what could happen next in a story or film.		
Get information from pictures, photos and charts in texts.		
Use the table of content pages and index of nonfiction books or texts.		
Use computer keyboard, software and programs confidently.		
Recognizeuppercaseandlowercaseletters and understand their role.		
Have significant phonological (sound) knowledge.		
Have some knowledge of the role of nouns, verbs, adjectives in sentences.		
Understand the role of punctuation and recognize the different types.		
Readaloudwithconfidenceandexpression. Readasif talking.		
Choose material for him/her to read or view.		

Find appropriate websites on the internet.		
Sub-vocalize or whisper when reading silently. This needs to be overcome.		
Leave out unknown words in a text to use context to determine the meaning of a word.		
Stop and self-correct when what is being read doesn't make sense.		
Use their knowledge of letter/sound relationships when trying to read or sound out an unknown word. Break words into syllables.		
Useinitialletters ofwords, picturesandcontent knowledge as cues to gainmeaning.		
Use dictionaries (online and off).		

Reading Behaviour Check List Three		
Does your child:	**Yes**	**Not Yet**
Enjoy reading as a self-selected activity. Read for pleasure, for information during the day.		
Read to you from familiar and unfamiliar texts.		
Share their writing with you.		
Read TV program lists/shopping lists and other every day reading texts		
Read newspapers and magazines.		
Read novels appropriate for his/her age and interests.		
Read and follow written instructions.		
Retell the main points of a viewed or written text. Can they give an opinion?		
Recognize the work of famous authors andillustrators relevant to their age &experience.		
Comment about selected authors or illustrators.		
Discuss contents of given texts and give an opinion.		
Understand that many people can contribute to the making of a book or text.		
Attempt to read unknown words using decoding strategies and context cues.		
Infer and predict from written and viewed texts.		

Have a significant sight vocabulary of commonly used words.		
Understandtheroleofpictures,charts, diagramsand maps to present information.		
Use the table of contents page and index pages of books.		
Use the keyboard on a computer.		
Recognize letters written in a variety of fonts.		
Uses phonological (letter-sound knowledge).		
Identify parts of speech (e.g. nouns, verbs, adjectives) in sentences.		
Uses appropriate punctuation, expression and pauses when reading aloud.		
Takes the initiative and selects materials for reading/viewing.		
Selects texts related to a given topic.		
Locatekeywords inwrittenandelectronictexts(TV, websites).		
Get information using different parts of a text(e.g. title page, index).		
Predict meaning from titles, illustrations and prior knowledge of a topic.		
Read silently from a chosen text for at least ten minutes.		
Skim and scan texts to work out the meaning.		
Stop and re-read and self-correct when the meaning of a text is disrupted.		
Soundout andapplyknowledge ofcommonletter patterns to decode words.		
Uses word segmentation and syllabification to make sense of the whole word.		
Use a dictionary to help check the meaning of words.		

BE A SPELLING CHAMPION

AYRE'S WORD LIST

HERE ARE 26 SECTIONS. The words are graded according to difficulty.
The words in this list were selected because it was believed if a student learns to spell all the words, they will have covered most spelling patterns and rules of English.

LEARN TO SPELL THESE WORDS

To learn to spell a word you:

- **LOOK AT IT**
- **SAY IT**
- **COVER IT**
- **WRITE IT**
- **CHECK IT**

1. me do
2. and go at on
3. it is she can see run
4. the in so no now man ten bed top
5. he you will we an my up last not us am good little ago old bad red
6. of be but this all your out time may into him today look did like six boy book
7. by have are had over must make school street say come hand ring live kill late let big mother three land cold hot hat child ice play sea
8. day eat sit lot box belong door yes low soft stand yard bring tell five ball law ask just way get home much call long love then house year to I as send one has some if how her them other baby well about men for ran was that his led lay
9. nine face miss ride tree sick got north white spent foot blow block spring river plant cut song winter stone free lake page nice end fall feet went back away paper put each soon came Sunday show Monday yet find
10. give new letter take Mr. after thing what than its very or thank dear west sold told best form far gave alike add
11. seven forget happy noon think sister cast card south deep inside blue post town stay grand outside dark band game boat rest east son help hard race cover fire age gold read fine cannot May line left ship train saw
12. pay large near down why bill want girl part still placed report never found side kind life here car word every under most made said work our more when from wind print air fill along lost name room hope same glad with mine
13. became brother rain keep start mail eye glass party upon two they would any could should city only where week first sent mile seem even without afternoon Friday hour wife state July head story open short lady
14. reach better water round cost price become class horse care try move delay pound behind around burn camp bear clear clean spell poor finish hurt maybe across tonight tenth sir these club seen felt full fail set

stamp light coming cent night pass shut easy
15. catch black warm unless clothing began able gone suit track watch dash fell fight buy stop walk grant soap news small war summer above express turn lesson half father anything table high talk June right date road March next indeed four herself power wish because world country meet another trip list people ever held church once own before know were dead leave early close flower nothing ground lead such many morning however mind shall alone order third push point within done body
16. trust extra dress beside teach happen begun collect file provide sight stood fix born goes hold drill army pretty stole income bought paid enter railroad unable ticket account driven real recover mountain steamer speak past might begin contract deal almost brought less event off true took again inform both heart month children build understand follow charge says member case while also return those office great Miss who died change wire few please picture money ready omit anyway
17. except aunt capture wrote else bridge offer suffer built center front rule carry chain death learn wonder tire pair check prove heard inspect itself always something write expect need thus woman young fair dollar evening plan broke feel sure least sorry press God teacher November subject April history cause study himself matter use thought person nor
January mean vote court copy act been yesterday among question doctor hear size December dozen there tax number October reason fifth
18. eight afraid uncle rather comfort elect aboard jail shed retire refuse district restrain royal objection pleasure navy fourth population proper judge weather worn contain figure sudden forty instead throw personal everything rate chief perfect second slide farther duty intend company quite none knew remain direct appear liberty enough fact board September station attend between public friend during through police until madam truly whole address request raise August Tuesday struck getting don't Thursday

19. spend enjoy awful usual complaint auto vacation beautiful flight travel rapid repair trouble entrance importance carried lose fortune empire mayor wait beg degree prison engine visit guest department obtain family favor Mrs. husband amount human view election clerk though o'clock support does regard escape since which length destroy newspaper daughter answer reply oblige sail cities known several desire nearly
20. sometimes declare engage final terrible surprise period addition employ property select connection firm region convict private command debate crowd factory publish represent term section relative progress entire president measure famous serve estate remember either effort important due include running allow position field ledge claim primary result Saturday appoint information whom arrest themselves special women present action justice gentleman enclose await suppose wonderful direction forward although prompt attempt whose statement perhaps their imprison written arrange
21. forenoon lose combination avenue neighbor weight wear entertain salary visitor publication machine toward success drown adopt secure honor promise wreck prepare vessel busy prefer illustrate different object provision according already attention education director purpose common diamond together convention increase manner feature article service injure effect distribute general tomorrow consider against complete search treasure popular Christmas interest
22. often stopped motion theater improvement century total mention arrive supply assist difference examination particular affair course neither local marriage further serious doubt condition government opinion believe system possible piece certain witness investigate therefore too pleasant
23. guess circular argument volume organize summon official victim estimate accident invitation accept impossible concern associate automobile various decide entitle political national recent business refer minute ought absence conference Wednesday really celebration folk

24. meant earliest whether distinguished consideration colonies assure relief occupy probably foreign expense responsible beginning application difficulty scene finally develop circumstance issue material suggest mere senate receive respectfully agreement unfortunate majority elaborate citizen necessary divide
25. principal testimony discussion arrangement reference evidence experience session secretary association career height
26. organization emergency appreciate sincerely athletic extreme practical proceed cordially character separate February immediate convenient receipt preliminary disappoint especially annual committee decision principle judgment recommend allege

PHONOGRAMS RECORD SHEET

Recognize the sounds the following PHONOGRAMS spell.

Colour each square when the letter-sound relationship/s are recognised

b /b/ **b**at	**c** /k/ **c**at /s/ **c**ent	**d** /**d**/ did	**f** /**f**/ fit	**g** /**g**/ get /**j**/ gem	**h** /**h**/ him	**j** /**j**/ jet /**dge**/ bridge
k /**k**/ king	**l** /**l**/ lamp	**m** /**m**/ man	**n** /**n**/ nan	**p** /**p**/pop	**qu** /**qu**/quit	**r** /**r**/ran
s /**s**/ us /**z**/ as	**t** /**t**/ tap	**v** /**v**/van	**w** /**w**/win	**x** /**ks**/fox	**y** /**y**/yet /**e**/baby /**i**/my	**z** /**z**/zip
a /**a**/at /**a**/navy /**o**/want **e** /**e**/-end /**e**/-she	**i** /**i**/ ink /**i**/ dime	**o** /**o**/ odd /**o**/open /**oo**/do /**oe**/toe	**u** /**u**/ cup /**u**/music /**oo**/put	**er** /**er**/her /**ir**/first /**ur**/burn /**or**/work /**ear**/early	**sh** /**sh**/dish /**ti**/nation /**si**/session /**ci**/facial	**ee** /**ee**/see /**ea**/sea
oo /**oo**/boot /**oo**/foot	**ch** /**ch**/such /**k**/school /**sh**/chivalry	**ng** /**ng**/ sang	**ea** /**e**/eat /**e**/head /**a**/break	**ar** /**ar**/far	**ck** /**ck**/neck	**ed** /**ed**/ graded /**d**/loved /**t**/wrecked
or /**or**/for	**wh** /**wh**/when	**oa** /**oa**/ boat	**ey** /**a**/they /**e**/key	**ei** /**e**/ conceit /**a**/veil /**i**/forfeit	**e** /**e**/field /**i**/pie /**e**/lilies	**igh** /**igh**/sigh

kn	gn	wr	ph	gh	si	ough
/**kn**/knot	/**gn**/gnat	/**wr**/wrap	/**f**/photo	/**g**/ghost	/**si**/session /**zh**/vision	/**o**/though /**oo**/ through /**uf**/rough /**of**/cough /**aw**/ thought /**ow**/ bough

Phonograms - Record Your Child's Progress Here

CONSONANTS

b	c	d	f	g	h	j

k	l	m	n	p	qu	r

s	t	v	w	x	y	z

SHORT VOWEL SOUNDS

a	e	i	o	u

DIGRAPHS

er	ir	ur	wor	ear

sh	ee	th	ay	ai

ow	ou	oy	oi	aw

au	ew	ui	oo	ch

ng	ea	ar	ck	ed

or	wh	oa	ey	ei

ie	igh	eigh	kn	gn

wr	ph	dge	oe	gh

ti	si	ci	ough

www.ingramcontent.com/pod-product-compliance
Lightning Source LLC
Chambersburg PA
CBHW080545170426
43195CB00016B/2687
9780648797777